The Brown-tail Moth, Euproctis Chrysorrhcea (L.). A Report on the Life History and Habits of the Imported Brown-tail Moth, Together With a Description of the Remedies Best Suited for Destroying It

August Busch

Pupils of Farm School, Thompson's Island, destroying winter webs of brown-tail moth, Dec., 1902.

THE BROWN-TAIL MOTH
EUPROCTIS CHRYSORRHŒA (L.).

A REPORT ON THE
LIFE HISTORY AND HABITS OF THE IMPORTED BROWN-TAIL MOTH,

TOGETHER WITH A

DESCRIPTION OF THE REMEDIES BEST SUITED
FOR DESTROYING IT.

BY
CHARLES H. FERNALD, A.M., PH.D., AND
ARCHIE H. KIRKLAND, M.S.

PUBLISHED UNDER THE DIRECTION OF THE STATE BOARD OF AGRICULTURE,
BY AUTHORITY OF THE LEGISLATURE.

BOSTON:
WRIGHT & POTTER PRINTING CO., STATE PRINTERS,
18 POST OFFICE SQUARE.
1903.

APPROVED BY
THE STATE BOARD OF PUBLICATION

Commonwealth of Massachusetts.

OFFICE OF THE MASSACHUSETTS STATE BOARD OF AGRICULTURE,
BOSTON, March 2, 1903.

I have the honor to submit herewith the special report on the life history and habits of the imported brown-tail moth (*Euproctis chrysorrhœa*), prepared under authority of chapter 42 of the Resolves of 1902. The work of preparing this report was delegated to Prof. C. H. Fernald and Mr. A. H. Kirkland, whose careful studies of the insect have made them entirely familiar with its habits. It has been the aim of the authors to present facts of practical value to the property owner, rather than technical details; and it is hoped that the report will help our citizens to a better understanding of the habits of the moth and methods for destroying it.

Respectfully submitted,

JAMES W. STOCKWELL.

THE BROWN-TAIL MOTH.

Nearly two centuries ago the famous French entomologist, Reaumur, wrote with delightful accuracy on the habits and life history of a caterpillar, which, from its wide distribution and frequent occurrence, he called "*la commune*," — the common caterpillar. He described the strange habit of the caterpillars in wintering half grown in a common web; their ravages in the spring in orchard and field, and their feeding, growth and transformation into white moths with bodies tipped with a golden band, — a marking that at once explains the more familiar name, "the brown-tail moth." This insect is indeed common in Europe, and occurs wherever the pear and apple flourish. In England, France and Germany its record is one of frequent damage to fruit and shade trees, to shrubs and flowering plants, while at intervals it has appeared in prodigious numbers, causing outbreaks that became matters of historical importance, and resulting in severe loss and grave alarm on the part of afflicted property owners.

Such, in brief, is the brown-tail moth: in summer, a snow-white, brown-tailed moth, laying its eggs on the leaves of pear and many other trees; in August, myriads of tiny caterpillars, feeding on the tender foliage at the tips of twigs; in winter, hibernating safely in a tight silken web; in spring, sallying forth to complete their growth on bud, blossom and leaf; in June, ending the life cycle in cocoons from which the moths emerge by the middle of July. A paragraph will give a synopsis of its known life history; a volume would not record its damage in the old world, or the full importance of its unfortunate introduction into the new; in fact, we do not know as yet just what rôle this insect is to play in our horticultural operations, how many crops it will attack with severity, or how far it will spread.

In the present report we have attempted to give a plain statement of what is known of the habits of this most injurious and annoying insect, with remedies best suited for its destruction. While the authors have collaborated throughout the entire work, the parts pertaining to the European history and the biology of the moth have been largely prepared by Professor Fernald, while the history of the moth in Massachusetts and the chapter on remedies have received special attention from Mr Kirkland. A large part of the experiments on the moth, and nearly all the field observations on its habits, were made by us under the direction of the gypsy moth committee in 1897-99; and to this committee, whose faithful labors have been of such signal value to the State, we are specially indebted for many favors in connection with this report.

Discovery of the Moth

In the spring of 1897 several residents of Somerville and Cambridge, Mass., found a strange caterpillar feeding on the unfolding leaves of pear trees. Apparently the insects came from small, tough webs at the tips of the twigs, particularly at the tops of the trees. They worked downward, consuming the foliage as they moved, and daily grew in size. By the time the foliage was two-thirds developed, the naked tree tops tipped with the gray abandoned webs were conspicuous objects in the infested district. The outbreak at that time was not widespread, but several thrifty property owners noticed with alarm the inroads the insects were daily making on the trees. When the damage by these insects was first observed, the campaign against the gypsy moth was being prosecuted vigorously under the auspices of the State Board of Agriculture, and the office of the gypsy moth committee at Malden naturally was regarded as an information bureau on all matters pertaining to insect depredations. Damage by the gypsy moth was well known, and dreaded correspondingly. Property owners finding new or strange insects on trees or crops frequently mistook them for gypsy moths, and requested information or help from the committee, in order to suppress the insects.

In this way Mr. Joseph B. Pike, living at 51 Preston Street, Somerville, Mass., noticing the work of the strange caterpillar, on May 8, 1897, sent word to the office of the gypsy moth committee that an insect which he supposed to be the gypsy moth was destroying his pear trees. This complaint was promptly investigated by an agent of the committee, Mr. Fletcher Osgood, who reported that an insect, presumably the tent caterpillar, was at work on the pear trees; and Mr. Pike was advised to spray the trees with some arsenical poison

A second complaint of damage was received May 14 from the well-known mycologist of Harvard University, Dr. Roland Thaxter, and similar injury to pear trees was observed. The unusual feature of a tent-making caterpillar at work in the spring on *pear* trees aroused the interest of Mr. Kirkland, at the time assistant entomologist to the gypsy moth committee Securing specimens, and not being able to identify the insects off hand, he commenced to rear them, in order that the species might be identified from the mature moths. Following Dr. Thaxter's complaint concerning the insect, other reports of damage came in rapidly to the gypsy moth office, and in the course of a few days it was evident that an insect outbreak of extraordinary nature was taking place in Somerville and Cambridge Specimens of the caterpillar were given to Prof. C H Fernald, entomologist to the committee, by Mr. Kirkland, who, being struck with the similarity of the habits of the caterpillars to those of the brown-tail moth as described in European literature, suggested to Professor Fernald that this new insect might possibly be that notorious pest. On his return to Amherst Professor Fernald compared the insects with figures and descriptions of the brown-tail moth in the European works, and at once was able to identify them as the brown-tail moth.

This identification promptly raised the interesting question of how these insects had become colonized in the locality where they were found. To obtain light on this point, careful examination of the infested district was made, and a number of owners of infested estates were interviewed. In this way a large amount of valuable information was obtained, but, as might be expected, a considerable part of it evidently pertained to depredations of insects other than the brown-tail moth. Eliminating these statements, there was still abundant evidence that the moth had been established in Somerville for several years previous to 1897, gradually becoming acclimated, and slowly spreading outward into non-infested territory. Many of these statements from owners of infested property were of especial interest, and it is well to record several of the more important at this point.

Mr. W. I. Chase, living at 85 Vine Street, Somerville, Mass., stated that he moved to his present place in 1892. In the spring of that year the caterpillars of the brown-tail moth defoliated a few pear trees, and then, driven by want of food, descended to the ground and attacked rhubarb and other plants, greatly injuring his garden crops. Since that date the caterpillars were more or less abundant each year, and in May, 1897, had stripped nearly all the fruit and shade trees on his place. Mrs. Chase stated that in the summer of 1896 the house and buildings adjacent "fairly swarmed with white moths."

Mr. J. A. Merrifield, 486 Somerville Avenue, Somerville, Mass., had noticed the webs of the brown-tail moth on his pear trees for at least three years preceding 1897, and up to that year had cut off and destroyed the webs each winter, thus applying of his own initiative the best remedy for preventing damage by the moth. As a result of this treatment, his trees were preserved from damage, while those of his neighbors were more or less defoliated. Owing to other duties in 1897, this work of web destruction was neglected until Patriot's Day, April 19, when they were destroyed as usual. This date proved too late, as the caterpillars had emerged and were crawling over the trees in great numbers, and as a result many of the trees were defoliated. Mr. Merrifield stated that he examined several webs April 1, and found that they contained masses of caterpillars, hence thought it safe to delay treatment until the holiday mentioned. Particular interest attaches to Mr. Merrifield's statement, as he is a conservative man, and possesses a good general knowledge of our common insect pests.

Mr. H. Foster, 23 Park Street, Somerville, Mass., removed and burned the tents on his trees each spring from 1895 to 1897. This was done before the caterpillars left the webs, and as a result his trees retained their foliage, while those of his neighbors were almost entirely defoliated.

Mr. John Walker, living at 2 Arnold Court, Somerville, Mass., stated that for more than three years previous to 1897 he had noticed damage by these caterpillars, the number of the insects increasing each year.

These statements indicate that the moth had been sufficiently numerous to cause noticeable injury since 1892-94. It is entirely probable that it occurred in small numbers for several years before it was noticed by property owners, so that it is safe to set the date of its introduction tentatively at about 1890. The question has been raised why the moth was not discovered at an early date by the employees of the gypsy moth committee. This is explained by the fact that in the part of Somerville where the moth was found the gypsy moth force had not worked for several years. Further than that, these men were obliged by law to confine their work to the gypsy moth, hence did not pay special attention to other insects unless they became injuriously abundant.

INTRODUCTION OF THE MOTH.

It seemed entirely probable that the place of the original introduction of the moth would be found in the worst-infested locality, as the insects would naturally increase in numbers and spread outward from year to year. An examination of the territory showed that the area of greatest damage was near the Somerville depot on the Fitchburg Railroad. Here by the middle of June the devastation had become truly formidable. Pear and apple trees were entirely defoliated, shade trees suffered severely, while even shrubs and herbage were not exempt from the attacks of the ravenous insects. Travelling outward in any direction from this point as a centre the damage by the moth gradually grew less, until at a distance of between one and two miles the infestations of the moth were merely sporadic and localized. Within the badly infested area there were two establishments which, from an entomological stand-point, were of a highly suspicious character, viz., an old abandoned nursery and a large greenhouse and florist's plant

Realizing how easily the insects in their closely spun webs might have been imported on nursery stock, the old nursery was carefully examined and the history of importations there made was investigated. It appeared that the nursery had not been in active operation since about 1895, and many of the trees left standing in the old nursery rows had attained to a large size. Among the latter there were several large specimens of *Pyrus*, a genus particularly favored by the caterpillar. Had the insect been introduced here, the nursery, with its surrounding yards, containing numerous fruit trees of considerable age, would have offered ideal conditions for the multiplication of the moth, and here we would have found ample evidence of long-continued infestation. On the contrary, however, careful examination of the nursery and the surrounding estates showed less than a dozen trees infested by the caterpillars.

Owing to the unpopularity of the moth, questions tending to connect any one with its importation were necessarily made in a guarded manner. The second suspicious place, the florist's establishment, perhaps one-fourth of a mile from the nursery, was visited, and the proprietors were questioned indirectly with reference to their importations of foreign perennials or shrubs. It was found that previous to about 1890 these parties had made a feature of importing roses from Holland and France, growing them for a year or two in large plots in the rear of the greenhouses, and then marketing them. Immediately in the rear of these plots were two blocks of large, full-grown pear trees, and these trees were completely defoliated by the caterpillars, and had a history of repeated defoliations extending backward for three or four years. Now, it is well known that the brown-tail moth occurs both in Holland and France; that in these countries it is not an uncommon pest of roses, — in fact, it is frequently mentioned in literature as being one of the

Plate 2.

Large web of brown-tail moth on apple. This web was made by the
consolidation of several colonies and contained
2218 small caterpillars.

important pests of roses. We know that it spins its winter webs freely on the rose, and that rose bushes are always imported in the fall, winter or spring, while both the bushes and the insects are in a dormant condition. The fact that this greenhouse was in the centre of the worst moth-infested district, and in consideration of the facts previously enumerated, makes the circumstantial evidence strong that the brown-tail moth was brought to this locality accidentally on imported roses, escaped, and spread naturally throughout the district. This case is but another excellent illustration of how the agencies of commerce and the business intercourse between nations are fast bringing about a worldwide distribution of our principal insect pests.

"It is indeed a strange fatality that another European insect, closely related to the gypsy moth by habit and structure, should become accidentally imported to the same locality to which thirty years before a misguided scientist brought the gypsy moth. It would seem that the world is large enough to give each of these pests a separate 'sphere of influence.' That they were both transported across the Atlantic to the same locality by totally dissimilar agencies must stand as one of the remarkable entomological events of the century just closed."[*] Now that we know the habits of the caterpillars in spinning their webs on so many different shrubs and trees valued for their fruit or for ornamental purposes, it seems all the more remarkable that the insect was not imported years ago. Our long immunity from the pest is greatly to the credit of European nurserymen, and gives evidence of the care with which nursery stock is selected and prepared for export. There is of course danger that the moth may be accidentally disseminated in this country by Massachusetts nurserymen, — a danger which we believe they will carefully guard against, as they have been fully advised concerning the matter by our efficient State Nursery Inspector, Dr. H. T. Fernald.

---

[*] Kirkland, Report Massachusetts Horticultural Society, 1902.

THE BROWN-TAIL MOTH IN EUROPE.

The original home of the brown-tail moth is in Europe, where it occurs over the entire country except in the extreme north. Altum quotes Speyer to the effect that it is "distributed over the whole of central and southern Europe, extends into Algiers on the south and to the Himalayas on the east. The polar limit is in Sweden at 57°, the equatorial in the Himalayas at 34°." Kirby states that it is "common in central and southern Europe, north Africa and western Asia, but is a local insect in England." The moth has also been doubtfully reported from Japan. This wide distribution is significant, as indicating the ultimate probable range of the insect in the United States.

The literature of the brown-tail moth is as old as the literature of economic entomology. When man began to record his troubles with the pests of crops, this insect was among the first to receive attention. The remarkable outbreaks of the caterpillars in certain years created astonishment as well as alarm. Being clearly out of the established order of things, they were regarded as a punishment for human shortcomings, and as Divine interposition seemed to offer the only remedy, it was freely invoked to stay the plague. Thus in 1543, during an outbreak of the brown-tail moth, a member of the city council at Grenoble introduced a resolve begging the local church official "to excommunicate these pests and censure them, in order to check the damage they were doing daily." To the credit of the council, let it be added, the resolve was promptly enacted. In the same century, Chorier, a historian of Dauphiny, relates that these caterpillars were so abundant that the attorney-general of the province found it necessary to issue an injunction against them, and ordered them to evacuate the fields where they were feeding. Such records as these testify strongly to the early damage by the moth, and the helplessness of the farmers of that day in the face of the caterpillar outbreaks.

Goedart, writing in 1635, describes the "singular nature" and "remarkable knowledge and foresight" of the caterpillars in preparing their winter shelters. Madam Merian described the habits of the moth in 1683, and Albin in 1720. In 1731, Reaumur, travelling from Tours to Paris, "found every oak in possession" of these caterpillars, and later made very complete studies of their habits. Roesel, in 1746, mentions and describes the moth. Linnæus described the moth in his "Systema Naturæ," Vol. I., p. 502, 1758, and gave it the scientific name *Bombyx chrysorrhœa*. The genus *Bombyx* of Linnæus has been divided by later entomologists into a large number of genera, based on structural characters, and this species, forming the type of the new genus *Euproctis*, is now known by the scientific name of *Euproctis chrysorrhœa* (L.) Since the time of Linnæus the brown-tail moth has been figured and described by nearly every entomologist who has written on the moths of Europe, and more or less complete accounts have been given of its life history and habits.

Geoffroy, in his "Histoire abregée des Insectes," Vol. II., p. 117, 1762, in writing of the brown-tail moth in the vicinity of Paris, says that it is the most common of all caterpillars, and is found on almost all trees, which it often entirely defoliates in the spring.

In 1782, William Curtis published an account of the depredations of the brown-tail moth, in which he informs us that at that time "the inhabitants of London and its vicinity were thrown into the utmost consternation" at the hosts of caterpillars of this species, that completely stripped the trees and shrubs of their leaves for miles in many places. The general appearance was such as might well cause alarm, for plants, hedges and "whole plantations of fruit trees, as well as trees of the forest, shared in the general havoc, presenting their leafless branches in the midst of summer as though stricken and destroyed by the blasts of winter. An appearance so extraordinary was calculated to create terror; it was naturally interpreted as a visitation from heaven, ordained to destroy all the sources of vegetable life, to deprive man and cattle of their essential food, and finally leave them a prey to famine" (Donovan). The alarm of the public was so great and prevailed to such an extent that prayers were publicly offered in the churches to avert the calamity. Believing, doubtless, that in emergencies works are as necessary as faith, the town fathers offered a shilling per bushel for the caterpillar webs. These latter were cut off and burned "under the inspection of the church wardens, overseers or beadle of the parish, at the first onset of this business, four score bushels, as I am credibly informed, were collected in one day, in the parish of Clapham" (Curtis)

Olivier, in 1790, mentions the insect as very common in the neighborhood of Paris, where it feeds "indifferently on all fruit trees and on nearly all other trees, one finds them as frequently in the forests as in the gardens."

Writing in 1803, Haworth, "Lepidoptera Britannica," p. 109, states that "the caterpillars of this insect have sometimes become so exceedingly numerous as to do incredible damage to the vegetable kingdom, and refers to the historic outbreak at London in 1782. Donovan, in his "British Insects," Vol. XVI, pp 39–45, 1813, gives a good general account of the habits and damage by the insect, and quotes freely from Curtis's pamphlet on the moth, — a work that has now become very rare. Bechstein, in "Forst u. Jagdw.," 4th, 2 Bd, 1818, describes the moth under the name of "white thorn spinner," from its habit of attacking this shrub. He writes "It is said that these caterpillars have devastated whole areas of forest, particularly oak wood lands. They are most injurious in the fruit garden." He notes that the caterpillars "in the spring gnaw the buds, blossoms and leaves, and strip even the second crop of leaves from the tree. They also destroy the fruit, and make the tree sickly through sap exhaustion.

J. B. Godart, "Hist Nat. des Lepidopteres," Vol. 4, p. 273, 1822, comments on the law which required French property owners to clear their trees of the winter webs, and expresses the belief that a better plan would be "to destroy the clusters of eggs immediately after they are laid," — a method which is of course wholly impracticable where large trees are infested. Blumenbach, 1825, considered this insect "one of the most destructive caterpillars to fruit trees," while four years later, M. Wallner, "Ann Soc Hort, 'Paris, Vol. 4, found the caterpillars causing severe damage throughout Bohemia, Austria, Bavaria and Switzerland, and urged the importance of destroying the mature moths.

Rennie, "Nat. Hist. Insects," p 266, 1830, tells us how the young caterpillars feed in ranks on the leaves. "the heads of each rank being generally in the same line, they all advance simultaneously, and their progress has very much the appearance of a regular military movement ' He gives as food plants the elm, white thorn, black thorn, oak and fruit trees. In 1832, Boisduval, "Coll Icon. des Chenilles d'Europe," records the caterpillar as extremely common, and doing "much damage to fruit trees, which are often stripped of their leaves." He points out the wisdom of destroying the winter webs in good season, before the caterpillars emerge, by burning them from the trees Again, in his "Entomologie Horticole," 1867, he states that this is the most common insect in France, and that it lives on all kinds of fruit trees and on nearly all forest trees

Ratzeburg, writing of this insect in Germany, in 1840, says that it is distributed over nearly all Europe, and is known everywhere as a pest both in the forests and orchards, where it often destroys the entire fruit crop and injures the shape of the trees. It frequently occurs in the forests in multitudes on the oaks, willows, elms and other deciduous trees, entirely devouring the leaves and blossoms. Writing at a subsequent date, he states that in the late '50's the caterpillars ravaged the oaks in the streets of Potsdam, and even killed some of them Brehm and Rossmassler, in their "Thiere des Waldes," 1867, write of the moth as being more injurious than certain allied species, and emphasize the need of web destruction These authors consider the brown-tail moth as being "more injurious in the fruit garden than in the forest." Figuier, "Insect World,' 1868, describes how the caterpillars have ravaged " the plantations of the promenades of Paris." Blanchere, "Ravageurs des Forets," 1876, writes pertinently of the folly of neglecting the destruction of the winter webs, his observations being as applicable to American as to French conditions Of the apathy of the average property owners he says "Thus they delay or neglect the most simple precautions up to the time a real invasion takes place, or until the frightful damage arouses their attention. Then the public clamor warns the local authorities. It disturbs them, and the government sends savants to observe the spread of the phenomenon, and at the same time to invent a remedy for this neglected evil. But the savants, arriving unfortunately in the midst of a bona fide outbreak, do nothing; for there is nothing to do, and the insignificant remedies attempted are too late, or amount to nothing. It is not during the time of severe epidemics to combat this pest, it is by an application of practical methods, established and followed carefully and patiently during many years.' Writing in 1881, Altum, " Forstzoologie, Vol. 3, p. 106, states that the nests of the moth were very abundant in the vicinity of Eberswald " in 1874–75, on isolated fruit trees, chiefly pear, the latter being thickly infested. . . . On older fruit trees there were as many naked branches as there were nests." In northern Germany "they are the chief plague of young oak forests, oak plantations, and particularly the lower-growing oaks." In Brehm's "Tierleben," Vol. 9, 1892, Taschenberg has written: " These caterpillars are in the first rank of those which affect our fruit trees, and not unfrequently through enormous outbreaks is shown the character of the inexcusable neglect of the orchardist who during the winter or early spring could so readily cut off and burn the easily found caterpillar nests.

Fischer, " Schlich's Manual,' Vol. 4, 1895, states that " in the Berlin Zoological Garden they [the caterpillars] destroy the foliage almost every year.' With reference to destroying the caterpillars he says " Care must be taken to protect the hands against the hairs, which cause inflammation." This damage at Berlin is also mentioned by an anonymous writer in " Gartenflora," p. 360, 1897, who says that the caterpillars " this spring have entirely stripped the oaks and many bushes in the Zoological Garden as well as in the Botanical Garden." These references, taken from the vast mass of foreign writings on the brown-tail moth, show how well the insect is known, and what a formidable pest it is at home.

Work of brown-tail moth caterpillars in Spring. Upper pear twig sprayed with arsenate of lead and protected; lower twig not sprayed.

From photo at Medford, Mass., May 17, 1899.

The 1897 Outbreak.

The 1897 outbreak of the brown-tail moth was a localized one, but made up in severity what it lacked in extent. A circle of two miles in diameter, with centre at the depot on Park Street, and including parts of Somerville and Cambridge, would contain nearly all of the devastated area. At Malden, Everett, and more particularly at Medford, there were small infestations, mainly of importance as indicating that the spread of the moth outward from the central colony had already begun, and affording insects for the infestation of new territory. In the central district the devastation was almost complete. The pear and apple trees, on which the majority of the winter webs had been spun, were first stripped. Such remarkably large numbers of these insects were harbored by these trees that their leaf supply was soon consumed, and the half-grown caterpillars were forced to migrate in search of food. In this migration shade trees suffered as severely as fruit trees from the attacks of the insects. Willows, elms, maples and lindens often were completely defoliated. In their mad search for food the insects swarmed along fences and sidewalks, making the latter slippery with their crushed bodies, and even entered houses. Rose bushes, grape vines, garden crops and even grasses were consumed by the hungry insects. By the middle of June the trees in the central infested district appeared as if swept by fire, the damage, so far as it went, being as severe as any caused by the gypsy moth.

This outbreak of the moth in 1897, now historic, is entitled to more than passing mention, since the scenes there enacted will doubtless be repeated many times as the moth spreads into new territory. In fact, such an outbreak is often necessary to arouse the average citizen from his apathy toward the care of trees, and make him see the wisdom and necessity of stamping out this particular pest wherever it occurs in any considerable numbers. While the details of the swarming of the caterpillars in 1897 are still well remembered by those who suffered from the moth, statements made by property owners soon after the outbreak are of special interest, and we reproduce a few of them, to give an adequate idea of the real significance and importance of this new pest of fruit and shade trees.

Statements from Citizens

Mrs. C. D. Chase, 18 Ivaloo Street, Somerville, says :—

We first noticed the brown-tail moth caterpillars in 1895. They were so close together they looked like brown fur. We found them on the trees and fences, in the house, and even found their cocoons on the window screens. In 1897 they were so thick we could not go out of doors without getting them on our clothing. The front of the house and the pear trees in the garden were covered with them. That summer the pear trees looked as if a forest fire had swept over them. The second brood did not seem to trouble us as much as the first. For the past two years we have not had any fruit, the trees blossomed this year, but the fruit dropped off.

Mrs. E. E. Bailey, 21 Medford Street, Malden, writes :—

I have lived here six years, and never noticed the moth until 1898. We did not have it in 1897. The pear trees were the only ones touched, but the caterpillars ate the leaves off from them. The leaves came out again, and there were some blossoms, but they did not blossom as they would if the leaves had not been eaten. Then the caterpillars came and ate the trees bare again, so that they looked as they do in winter. We did not get a bit of fruit from any of them this year. The house was covered with these caterpillars, and they even came into my kitchen. I had to gather them up and burn them. I used to sweep them up by hundreds and burn them with oil.

Nicholas Fleming, corner of Kent and Beacon streets, Somerville, says :—

We first noticed the brown-tail moth two years ago (1896). We got no fruit that year, and we have not had a pear this year. The stripping did not seem to kill the trees, they leaved out again. My sons spent all the spare time they had in picking off the caterpillars and killing them with kerosene. This summer the insects bothered us considerably in the apple trees. The currant bushes were eaten both years. A small grape-vine was badly eaten, and the caterpillars also attacked the peach tree. For two years we have had almost no fruit. This spring the boys took off the nests and trimmed the trees, and that has saved them.

Vincent L. Kelly, 33 Park Street, Somerville, writes: —

We first noticed the brown-tail moth in May, 1897. That year we had no fruit, and we have had none this year. The trees were entirely stripped (1897), but came out again later. Some time about the middle of June the caterpillars began to disappear. While they were with us they were a most disgusting sight. They clung to the outside of the house and piazza, and some even got into the house. We tried killing them by picking them off the fences, etc., and putting them into kerosene, but we could not accomplish much, as they were so numerous.

Mrs. Peter Mooley, 41 Ivaloo Street, Somerville, says: —

We first noticed the caterpillars in 1897, and we could do nothing with them. We had to take brooms and sweep them away from the doors. They ate the leaves off the trees, so that we did not get any fruit that year or in 1898. The caterpillars seemed to come all at once. We were all poisoned with them. The houses were full of them. They were a sight. They were on everything, — fences, shrubbery and flower bushes. The place was fairly alive with them. They were even in the bed-rooms. We tried lime and salt, but nothing seemed to check them.

Mrs. H. F. Williams, 213 Beacon Street, Somerville, states: —

The caterpillars were very bad in 1897. They would have stripped the trees if we had not fought them, even then they damaged the trees. In spite of all we could do, they crawled all over the house, up to the door, and even got into the house. They seemed to be everywhere. We burned them to get rid of them. They did not destroy our trees, but it was only because we attended to them all the time. They would have eaten the trees in one night, if we had not kept them down. The trees did not bear at all this year (1898), and we have had no fruit but cherries. The caterpillars ate everything that came within their reach, — rose bushes, geraniums and plants. Nothing was free from them but the grape-vines. They were not so numerous this summer as last. All the nests were supposed to have been taken

… that there were a good many left. I think most
… summer came from a family across the way.
… pestered with them. They did what they could
… could not keep them down.

Mr. D. J. Chase, Somerville, says:—

In … 1896 I first noticed the brown-tail moth on
… The caterpillars did not do any particular damage
… the millers came out thick. In 1897 the cater-
… in such numbers they destroyed everything. I
… any special pains to get rid of them until after they
… everything. We had no fruit that year, and we
… 1898. While feeding, the caterpillars would
… leaves, fruit buds and all. In 1896 only one small tree
… the next year they attacked the cherry, elm, pear
… trees. They came into the house, the walks and fences
… covered with them. For three or four days I went out
… and swept them off the planks. Last winter I cut
… buds so that we did not have any this year. Gener-
… my neighbors took care of their trees, though there
… I not.

Ernest J. Doherty, 640 Somerville Avenue, Somerville,
says:—

In May 1897 the brown-tail moth caterpillars came out in
… devoured everything,—leaves, blossoms and all;
… about two months. I didn't have any chance to take
… trees—they got ahead of me. One Sunday the men
… on them all day, killing and burning them. I
… caterpillars on the fences, crawling over into the
… to the railroad; they were crawling everywhere.
… they gathered themselves into the leaves and
… of the house. This year they got into the grape-vine
… for two years. Two small apple trees died,
… being enough to stand the stripping.

Mr. C. J. Kennerston, 17 Park Street, Somerville, says:—

In … 1897 ate all the leaves off my trees, and we
… with the exception of two or three pears that
… fruit on constant at all. The trees were old, and
… to beat them. After the leaves came out the

Plate 4.

Pear tree defoliated by the caterpillars of the brown-tail moth. The webs on the trees in the back-ground were destroyed during the previous winter. Photo taken at Vine Street, Somerville, May 27, 1897.

trees suddenly looked as though they had been burned by fire. That summer all the foliage around here seemed to be scorched I would leave home in the morning, and the trees would be budding out, the next day they would be stripped clean The caterpillars were all around the house, on the fence and even in the house. I could not go into the yard without having them drop on me from the trees I think the brown-tail moths are worse than the gypsy moths.

Mrs. J Leland, 377 Washington Street, Somerville, says —

The brown-tail moth caterpillars came in large numbers, they stripped all of our trees My son got the nests off some of the trees, but the trees he was not able to clear were just eaten up, and we did not have any fruit We had no fruit to speak of for two years, except on one tree which was right near the house, that we were able to keep clean of nests. The insects were very destructive I think they killed my strawberry plants My rose bushes were somewhat eaten, too They ate the elms across the street, and then came over to my rose bushes We had a second crop of the caterpillars They ate the leaves on grape-vines, pear and apple trees. I think they are the worst creatures I ever saw We could not sit in our garden without having them crawl all over us They will even eat the vegetables growing in the garden, they ate the beet tops and cabbages I think they are much worse than the gypsy moth, because they increase so fast There are enough caterpillars in one nest to cover a whole tree, and there will be a dozen or twenty nests on a tree.

Mrs. J. A. Kincaid, 88 Vine Street, Somerville, writes —

We first noticed the brown-tail moth in 1897, when they stripped the trees so that they looked as though they had been burned They stripped them twice that year We have not had an apple or a pear from them since They blasted all the rose buds we had. We would have been satisfied if they had taken the rest of the pear trees, for they are now no good A few came into the house, perhaps two or three, and we found one in the bed The caterpillars came in droves right down the driveway I am not exaggerating when I say that our fence and the gate posts were so covered with the caterpillars that they looked as though they were covered with fur We poured kerosene oil over them, and had to keep that gate closed all summer, because there was a tree near it

would not lease property so located, while those occupying houses near which the caterpillars were abundant often were forced to vacate the same. Mr. L. L. Tower, of the Tower-Cutter Company, Boston, writes us:—

The year before the brown-tailed moth appeared in my pear orchard at Somerville it produced over two hundred bushels of pears, the next year the caterpillars were on the trees by the bushel, and I did not have a pear that or the following year. The damage by the caterpillars was a great annoyance, not only to my tenants but to the neighbors. As a consequence, my tenants moved out and left the house vacant for about a year.

Mrs. E. Gibson, 72 Beacon Street, Somerville, says:—

We were all badly poisoned by these moths. We did not know that they were here when we took the house, and so we have had to bear the consequences. My husband spoke to the owner of these premises, and told him that unless something was done we could not stay. He said he knew they were dreadful things to have around, but did not seem to be able to do anything. The trees were eaten up by them, and we had no fruit whatever. They troubled us more or less all summer. They seemed to be worse here than anywhere, but all our neighbors were troubled with them and tried to get rid of them. The trees and grass were covered with them. We used to take brooms and try to sweep them off the piazza, and we had to guard against them getting into the house. They were a regular plague.

Mrs. Alexander Garbota, 160 Park Street, Somerville, says:—

The first time these caterpillars troubled us was in 1897, and then they were terrible. Everyone about here complained of them. They were not only outside but inside the house. I found them on my pillows. One of my tenants moved away on account of them. My tenant who lived up stairs could not open her windows. The caterpillars were all over her piazza, and she could not sit there because of them. She would brush the caterpillars up with the broom into a good pile, and then call me to look at them, and I would have to hold the pan while she swept them up, and then we carried them to the back yard and burned them. This was very bad for me, and poisoned me dreadfully. My neck was all swollen up and red with a rash.

The testimony of such witnesses gives unquestioned evidence of the damage caused by the moth. A large number of statements equally interesting and of the same general tenor have been omitted, as being only corroboratory. Public interest in the moth was most intense wherever the insect had appeared in force; trees were devastated, garden crops destroyed, and dwellings swarmed with the caterpillars; while to the gypsy moth committee and their employees went forth in no uncertain tones the Macedonian cry, "Come over and help us,"— an appeal to which the committee did not turn a deaf ear.

The 1897 outbreak was novel and even alarming, hence property owners observed the caterpillars more closely than in later years; yet each year since in sections where the moth has been neglected the same devastation of trees, the same migrating of hungry caterpillars, the same injury to human beings, has occurred. Wherever web destruction at the proper time has been properly carried out, either by individuals or municipalities, a notable degree of freedom from damage by this insect has been secured.

The Campaign against the Moth.

As soon as the identity of the brown-tail moth had been settled, the infested district was thoroughly examined by Messrs. Fernald and Kirkland, accompanied by President H. H. Goodell of the Hatch Experiment Station of the Massachusetts Agricultural College. Appreciating the gravity of the situation, President Goodell authorized the preparation of a special bulletin on the insect, which was published by the Hatch Experiment Station in July, 1897, and generally distributed in the metropolitan district. The presence of the moth was also brought to the attention of His Excellency the late Governor Roger Wolcott, by the following letter from the gypsy moth committee and the director of the Experiment Station: —

Boston, May 25, 1897.

His Excellency Roger Wolcott, *Governor of the Commonwealth.*

Sir, — We desire to submit for your consideration the facts relative to another insect pest which has appeared for the first time in this Commonwealth and in the United States.

Plate 5.

Pear tree stripped by brown-tail moth caterpillars,
Medford, Mass., May 17, 1899.

It is commonly called the brown-tail moth (*Euproctis chrysorrhœa*), and is so destructive in its habits, having so wide a range of food, that in European countries it is one of the few insects for the suppression of which laws have been enacted

The centre of the infested district in this State appears to be in Somerville, though how widely the insect is dispersed we have been unable to determine in the short time intervening since its appearance. In an examination of the district by our entomologist, Prof. C. H Fernald, and Dr. L. O Howard, chief of the Division of Entomology, Department of Agriculture, Washington, D. C., the insect was found feeding on the pear, apple, cherry, strawberry, raspberry and rose bushes. The trees were entirely stripped of their leaves, and the trunks, fences and sidewalks were swarming with the caterpillars.

The side of a house in the vicinity was covered with them, and they had even pushed their way into the interior. The most seriously affected point is immediately around the depot and railway tracks, increasing greatly the risk of dispersion.

The caterpillars are just finishing their feeding state, and will soon go into the pupa condition. The time to attack them is now, by contact insecticides, and in the late summer when they emerge.

Dr Howard, government entomologist, now here inspecting our work on the gypsy moth, has kindly consented to give the benefit of his advice.

To meet this sudden emergency, a special appropriation of $10,000 from the Legislature seems absolutely necessary, and we therefore beg Your Excellency to take such steps as seem in your judgment best.

      E W Wood,
      Augustus Pratt,
      S S Stetson,
      John G Avery,
      F. W. Sargent,
      Wm R Sessions,
   Committee of the Board of Agriculture
    on Gypsy Moth, Insects and Birds

      Henry H Goodell,
    Director Hatch Experiment Station

The matter was also presented to the Governor orally by the gypsy moth committee, Messrs Fernald and Kirkland, with Dr. L. O Howard, entomologist of the United States Department of Agriculture, who fortunately was in Boston at

THE BROWN-TAIL MOTH

On May 27 it was brought to the attention of the Senate by special message from Governor Wolcott [...] was referred to the agricultural committee, and [...] committee through Representative W. H. [...] reported a bill placing the work of de[struction of the] brown-tail moth in the hands of the gypsy [moth commit]tee and appropriating $6,000 for the needs [...]. On June [...] the ways and means committee [reported adv]ersely on the bill. Later in the session a bill [presented] by Col. Albert Clarke of Wellesley, and requiring [local au]thorities to suppress the moth, was passed to be en[acted] and is presented in full below:—

CHAPTER 386, ACTS OF 1897.

AN ACT TO REQUIRE LOCAL AUTHORITIES TO SUPPRESS THE BROWN TAIL MOTH.

1. Whenever the pest known as the brown tail moth appears in any city or town of the Commonwealth it [shall be the duty] of the city or town government to take immediate [steps for its] extinction and to prevent its spread. If they [are in doubt whether] the pest is [present] they shall notify the board of agriculture, [and if] they are informed by said board that such [pest exists in their] respective municipalities they shall at once [begin the] work of its confinement to the infested area and its [extinction].

2. It shall be the duty of the board of agriculture to [cause investigations to] be made upon the receipt of notice from local [authorities and] also whenever the board has reason to suspect [the presence of the] pest in any city or town, and to furnish the [latter with ample] supply of printed directions as to the [methods of] confinement and extinction.

3. [It shall be the] duty of the owners and managers of [lands infested by] this moth to exert themselves persistently to [suppress] it under the direction of local and state [authorities and to] promptly report any spread of the pest which [...]

4. Mayors and aldermen of cities and selectmen of [towns who] refuse to comply with the requirements [of this act on] information or complaint of the district attorney [shall be indict]ed by the grand jury, and on conviction of such [offense shall] be fined ten dollars each for every day of

such neglect or refusal after the receipt of due notice from the board of agriculture that their city or town is thus infested

SECTION 5 The owner or manager of any infested premises who shall, after the receipt of a notice in writing from the mayor and aldermen of his city or from the selectmen of his town, or from the board of agriculture, neglect or refuse to comply with this act, shall upon conviction of such neglect or refusal, before any court of competent jurisdiction, be fined one dollar for every day of such neglect, or confined in jail not more than five days nor less than one day, or suffer both penalties in the discretion of the court

SECTION 6 This act shall take effect upon its passage   [Approved June 11, 1897.

In the mean time, the caterpillars were swarming in large numbers along the line of the Fitchburg Railroad at Somerville, and were evidently being scattered on trains. A few of the employees of the gypsy moth committee therefore were detailed to stamp out this pest spot, and this was done, the caterpillars being destroyed by spraying with soap solutions and kerosene emulsion. On June 24, 1897, the executive committee of the Board of Agriculture voted to advise the mayors of Somerville, Cambridge, Malden, Medford and Everett that the brown-tail moth had become colonized in their respective municipalities, and urging them to take means to secure its suppression. It was also voted to spend a sum not to exceed $150 in examining towns thought to be infested. As a result, it was found that the moth had already become widely dispersed. The result of the examination made in the fall of 1897 is given below —

Infested Estates

Somerville,	1,111	Winchester,	24
Cambridge,	355	Woburn,	19
Medford,	149	Charlestown,	7
Malden,	92	Belmont,	3
Everett,	72	Burlington,	3
Melrose,	31	Saugus,	2
Stoneham,	31	Revere,	1
Arlington,	29		

It is probable the moth was distributed elsewhere at the time of this inspection, which from lack of funds was neces-

only a limited one. More or less activity was shown on the part of municipalities in suppressing the moth in the spring of 1898, especially in stamping out the worst infestations in Somerville and Cambridge. June 20, 1898, the law relating to the brown-tail moth was amended, and the following law enacted: —

[CHAPTER 541, ACTS OF 1898.]

AN ACT TO REQUIRE THE STATE BOARD OF AGRICULTURE TO TAKE CHARGE OF THE WORK OF EXTERMINATING THE BROWN-TAIL MOTH.

Be it enacted, etc., as follows:

SECTION 1. Whenever the pest known as the brown-tail moth appears in any city or town of this Commonwealth, it shall be the duty of the state board of agriculture to take immediate measures to prevent its spread; and, in the discharge of the duty imposed upon said board by this act, said board is hereby vested with all powers now conferred upon it by law in exterminating the gypsy moth, and may expend of the money heretofore appropriated for the extermination of the gypsy moth a sum not exceeding five thousand dollars.

SECTION 2. Any person who purposely resists or obstructs said state board of agriculture, or any person or persons in its employ, when engaged in the execution of the purposes of this act, shall be punished by a fine not exceeding twenty-five dollars for each offence.

SECTION 3. It shall be unlawful for any person knowingly to transport the insect known as the brown-tail moth, or its nests or eggs, within this Commonwealth, or for any person knowingly to transport said insect or its nests or eggs from any town or city to another town or city in this Commonwealth, except while engaged in work for the purposes of destroying them. Any person who violates the provisions of this section shall be punished by a fine not exceeding one hundred dollars, or by imprisonment in the house of correction not exceeding sixty days, or by both said fine and imprisonment.

SECTION 4. Chapter five hundred and sixteen of the acts of the year eighteen hundred and ninety-seven is hereby repealed. [*Approved June 20, 1898.*

It was sought to push the work of suppressing the moth directly under the control of the gypsy moth committee. It was decided to delay active measures until the fall, when a campaign of web destruction was commenced, in which large masses of webs, particularly in Cambridge, Somerville, Malden, Medford and Everett, were destroyed, the sum of $9,998.96 being spent in this work. Up to Jan. 1, 1899, thirty-two cities and towns were found infested by the moth.

Work against the brown-tail moth was continued by legislative enactment with another appropriation of $10,000, deducted from the sum appropriated for work against the gypsy moth. This was chiefly spent in web destruction late in the fall, the actual sum expended in this work being $9,999.81.

During the year 1899 the following work was accomplished: —

Trees inspected,	413,758
Trees sprayed,	2,517
Old winter webs destroyed,	13,519
New winter webs destroyed,	884,480

With the cessation of the State work against the gypsy moth and brown-tail moth, in February, 1900, it became necessary for municipalities to enter upon a campaign against the latter insect.

This work was taken up in good spirit by the worst-infested municipalities, and has been carried out to a greater or less extent each winter since that time. Cambridge, Somerville, Medford and Lynn have been particularly active in destroying the brown-tail moth, and as a result these cities have been quite generally exempt from damage by these caterpillars in the summer season. These operations have been largely directed toward the destruction of the moth on street trees. Many cities have taken the broad — and it seems to the writers entirely correct — view that the moth on private estates, if neglected, is a menace to the shade trees of the city as well as to the property of other citizens. Where this view has been held, the moth has been destroyed on street trees and private trees alike and, as a result of this treatment, cities like Somerville and Cambridge have gained quite a degree of immunity from the insect. Unfortunately, however, where certain cities fight the moth in a

THE BROWN-TAIL MOTH

[text largely illegible] intelligent manner, adjoining municipalities [...] the moth entirely, or combat it only [...] manner. This has resulted in undoing each [...] part of the good work accomplished in localities [...] freed from the moth. This state of affairs gives [...] reason for the necessity of thorough systematic [work] over the entire district, if the moth is to be [suppressed].

Painful Nettling from the Caterpillars

[Coincident] with the swarming of the caterpillars along [sidew]alks and on house walls, a very painful cutaneous [affection dev]eloped among citizens of the worst-infested districts. This affection developed usually on the hands, face [and] spread rapidly, and produced an intolerable itching. [At first the cause] of the trouble was not recognized by the [physicians] and some anxiety was felt, at least on the [part of the sufferers], lest a new epidemic disease had made [its appearance]. It was soon traced, however, to its proper [source], the hairs of the brown-tail moth caterpillar. This [sort of an insect] outbreak is so unusual in America that [it is worthy] of particular mention. Briefly stated, it was [found that] however the living caterpillars, or even the [cast cater]pillar skins formed in molting or spinning the [cocoon, came in cont]act with the human flesh, the eruption [was a natur]al but painful sequence.

[The nettling of] the human skin by caterpillars is not an [uncommon occurrence], but insects causing it, other than the [brown-tail moth, are] fortunately rare. One of our large [caterpillars not] uncommon on ash and apple, the larva of [...] is armed with spines that poison [...] the same holds true with the southern saddleback (*Empretia stimulea*). The injury in [both cases is com]parable to the stinging of bees or wasps, [the poisonous hairs] gaining entrance beneath the skin. [Other in]stances of nettling from caterpillar hairs are [those of] the hickory caterpillar (*Halesidota* [...]) the white-marked tussock moth (*Notolophus leu[costigma*). The injury] from the hairs of these insects is not to be compared in point of severity with that caused by the hairs of the brown-tail moth caterpillar, which is of a peculiarly intense, burning character. So far as known to us, no American insect can compare with it in this respect, although it is probably exceeded in severity by the urtication caused by the processionary caterpillar of Europe (*Thaumetopœa processionea*).

In orchards where there are large numbers of brown-tail moth cocoons, a light breeze is sufficient to waft the irritating hairs upon passersby, with most annoying and painful results. In investigating the habits of these caterpillars in the field we were often severely nettled by the hairs, and can testify that the intense irritation lasts for several weeks. The principal sufferers from this feature of the caterpillar outbreaks are women or children, who by necessity or habit are often confined quite closely to badly infested estates. Among these parties the suffering frequently beggared description.

Statements from Sufferers

Mrs. H. F. Williams, 213 Beacon Street, Somerville, says:—

We were shockingly poisoned by the caterpillars of the brown-tail moth. They troubled us all summer. Every member of my family was poisoned. At first we did not know what they were. My little boy could not go near them without getting poisoned, every time he went to pick cherries he would come down from the tree badly poisoned. If my baby went near where they were, his face would break out into a rash. I was so dreadfully poisoned that I thought I had some frightful disease. My hands, face, neck, arms and limbs were broken out with this rash. Most of the caterpillars we had in 1898 came from a neighbor's place. They came over the fence, into the house and even into the closets. They would get on clothes hung on the line, and when these were worn they poisoned us.

Mrs. E. L. Bailey, 21 Medford Street, Malden, writes:—

I was badly poisoned on my neck and arms by the caterpillars. At times I was nearly crazy with the itching and irritation caused by the poison, and one of my children was affected in the same way.

Mr. Daniel E. Chase, a well-known Somerville citizen, has written us: —

My whole family suffered from poisoning by these creatures, the skin being so badly irritated that we were obliged to bathe in soda water, salt water, etc. We felt the effects of the poisoning all summer. When my house was painted, the painters, in scraping under the eaves, started up the hairs of the caterpillars, and we were thus all more or less poisoned again.

Mrs. J. Leland, 377 Washington Street, Somerville, says: —

The caterpillars are very dangerous because they are so poisonous. They seem to poison everything they touch. We had to wash all vegetables brought in from the garden. My son, who worked in the garden a great deal, was badly poisoned, his neck was a solid mass of rash. The rest of the family were also poisoned in a less degree.

Miss McMahon, living at 632 Somerville Avenue, Somerville, says: —

We first noticed the caterpillars in 1897. They were all over the trees. At the same time we began to have a dreadful itching, from which we suffered so much that we were obliged to consult a physician.

A Typical Experience

A typical experience with the caterpillars is described by Mrs. C. D. Chase, living at 18 Ivaloo Street, Somerville: —

While cutting the limbs from the infested trees my husband was badly poisoned, his eyes in particular being affected. In cleaning the window screens in the house I was also badly poisoned, the skin of my body was as much inflamed as if a mustard paste had been applied. The poisoning did not seem to come entirely from contact, but the air seemed to be filled with something which caused the itching and burning sensation. We were affected during the whole two months that the insect was in the larval stage. In 1897, while the house was being painted, the painters all suffered more or less. Their distress was so great that they were obliged to stop their work and bathe the face, hands and arms with soda water to get relief. We could not hang out the clothes, as the hairs would cling to them, especially to the flannels, and when worn they would badly irritate the skin.

Plate 6.

Fig 1

Fig 2

Fig 3

Fig 4

Fig 5

Explanation of Plate

Figures Nos. 1, 2, 4 and 5 drawn from nature by J. H. Emerton

No. 1 — Female brown-tail moth
No. 2 — Winter web of brown-tail moth caterpillars
No. 3 — Pruning shears suitable for removal of winter webs
No. 4 — Brown-tail moth caterpillars, enlarged
No. 5 — Brown-tail moth caterpillars, natural size

Mrs. J. A. Chabot, 15 Park Street, Somerville, states: —

We were all badly poisoned by the caterpillars. We could not go into the yard without getting the irritation on the neck and arms, although we covered ourselves up as well as we could, in order to escape them. The man who took care of the yard was badly poisoned. Only a few caterpillars got into the house, but I suppose they came in on our clothing. This spring, when putting the screens on the windows, I noticed some of the cocoons on the clapboards, and scraped them off. As a result, my neck became badly poisoned.

Nicholas Fleming, corner of Kent and Beacon streets, Somerville, says: —

The poisoning by the caterpillars was truly dreadful. Every time we went into the yard we had to protect ourselves about the neck and head, to keep them off.

Mr. C. E. Kenniston, 17 Park Street, Somerville, writes: —

Both myself and family were greatly troubled by the sting or bite of these caterpillars. It seemed as if they poisoned us whenever we went near one of them. The webs made by the insects seemed to be poisonous. We had an awful time with them, and my son's face and hands were so badly puffed up that he had to call in a doctor.

Mrs. W. I. Chase, 85 Vine Street, Somerville, a most intelligent observer of the habits of the moth, states: —

In 1897 the caterpillars poisoned us terribly, and even now, when we go out and sweep down the sides of the house where the cocoons are, we get poisoned in the same way. While putting a new roof on the house my husband was nearly wild from the pain, and my neighbors tell me that every time they wash their windows they are poisoned.

Mrs. J. A. Kincaid, 88 Vine Street, Somerville, says: —

Our whole family was badly poisoned by the caterpillars. It took us all summer to get rid of the poison. Even now (October, 1898), when we get overheated the poison breaks out again on our bodies. One of my neighbors was so unfortunate as to get poisoned in one of her eyes, and had a hard time.

Miss West of 42 Preston Street, Somerville, on returning home from an absence of several weeks, —

was badly poisoned by the caterpillars. I had not been home twenty-four hours before I was poisoned. I did not know that the insects had gotten on me, and at first thought I had the measles. The trouble lasted for several weeks, and then gradually wore away.

Henry Foster, 23 Park Street, Somerville, says —

The caterpillars did not poison us until they got very thick. I suffered badly with them, I could not get rid of them, and changing my clothing seemed to do no good. Our neighbors were troubled more than we were. One of them was so ill that she had to call a physician.

J. A. Merrifield, previously quoted, states —

In 1897 we were much bothered by the poisoning of the caterpillars. You could not sit under the trees ten minutes before you would begin to feel the itching sensation. You might not find a caterpillar on you anywhere, but it would be only a few minutes before you would begin to itch.

Mrs. J. O'Connell, 82 Beacon Street, Somerville, says —

This summer whenever we sat under the trees we would have a terrible itching. The caterpillars poisoned me very badly. My hands, arms and face were covered with rash, and my children were broken out in the same way.

A Severe Case of Poisoning

From the nature of his work, Granville A. Walker, 9 Loring Street, Somerville, became badly poisoned by the insect, his case being one of the most severe in the devastated district. It is of particular interest, since the nettling came not from the caterpillars, but from the cocoons spun on house walls. He has written us —

I was painting a house on Vine Street in July, 1897. There were some caterpillars on the trees and many webs containing cocoons. Some of the branches were so near the house we were obliged to cut them off. The house was covered with cocoons also. We found them under the clapboards, and of course had to brush them off. My wrists and arms were poisoned, and soon became a sight. Some of my men were also badly affected, and all of them were more or less poisoned. It was terrible, — simply terrible! I had to go to a doctor for relief, and he gave me an ointment to allay the irritation. A neighbor of mine whose family had suffered severely from the poison of the brown-tail moth suggested the application of alcohol, as it had relieved her. This neighbor stated that each week they were freshly poisoned by the clothes, which, hanging on the line, came in contact with the hairs of the caterpillars; as a result, the skin was irritated when the clothes were worn.

In my own case, not only were my arms and wrists poisoned, but my whole body. The alcohol allayed the irritation so that I could get a little sleep, but the trouble lasted over a month, and was simply torture, the heat greatly intensifying the suffering. If I had known about it, I would not have painted the house for double the price of the job.

A more serious case, no doubt complicated with other ailments, has been described to us by Mrs. John H. McGarr, 80 Vine Street, Somerville, as follows: —

I first noticed the brown-tail moth in May, 1897. My mother discovered it, and called my attention to it. She saw the little caterpillars crawling about, and began killing them; but the more she killed, the more numerous they seemed to grow. Soon little white blisters began to come out upon her neck, and at last, about the 20th of May, she became very sick and we were obliged to get her away from here, because she was in such a bad state. The poison seemed to affect her entire body. After she had gone I became quite sick, also, and could not stay here, but was obliged to be removed. I was quite weak from the irritation caused by the eruption. When I scratched the irritated spots, little blisters would form. The doctor who was called in to attend my mother said they had poisoned her blood. She grew worse, and finally died of this poison about the middle of August. The doctor said her age was against her recovery, but she was a remarkably well-preserved woman, and in fairly good health before this occurrence. My son also was taken quite sick, and finally became so ill that he also had to be removed from this house. Everything I touched in the house seemed to be poisoned by the caterpillars. When the cold weather came I began to get better, but I have never entirely recovered from the effects of the poison. We had the moth again in 1898, but it was not a circumstance to what it ever had been the previous year. No one who had not seen it would believe what a scourge it was in 1897. When my husband came home and put on his clean flannels, he said they made him almost crazy. The caterpillars probably got into them as they hung on the line. The insects were all over the house, and the trees were a terrible sight.

Statements from Physicians.

So severe was the suffering caused by these insects that the services of physicians were in frequent demand. Statements from doctors living in the infested district and treating a great many cases of caterpillar "poisoning" are of particular interest, as giving an accurate summary of the matter from the medical stand-point. Two well-known physicians of large experience have kindly given us the statements which appear below.

George E. Osgood, M.D., 283 Highland Avenue, Somerville, writes: —

The past summer (1898) I have had, in round numbers, fifty cases of what is called dermatitis, or skin disease produced by the brown-tail moth. Wherever the hair strikes the skin it causes either small or large blotches. It even goes so far as to produce blebs, an affection of the skin which varies from a little red spot up to a large pustule, with pus or matter in it. The first attack lasts about a week, but one can be poisoned just as many times as the hair touches the skin. The after-effects seem to be trivial, unless a person has tuberculosis or dropsy. In a dropsical patient it is very bad, aggravating the trouble. On Summer Street I had three cases of poisoning in one family, and on Spring Hill Terrace I had cases in seven houses. I protected myself from the affection by using disinfectants after being near the moth. I find that people with light complexions are affected, apparently, more than those of dark complexions. By the former it seems to be absorbed by the system, and the lymphatics are swollen. I do not know of a case where the lymphatics have been enlarged in a person with dark complexion. In 1897 there seemed to be less trouble from poisoning than in 1898. I had but about fifteen cases. We have had quite a number of the moths about our place this year, although we had the trees thoroughly cleaned last fall. We have found them crawling up the trees, making their cocoons in them and under the eaves of the house.

Dr. O. A. Gibson, 22 Summer Street, Somerville, writes: —

The first we saw of these moths was in 1897. The first cases of poisoning I saw were on Spring Hill Road and Park Street. I saw a number of cases, and they were all about the same, except that they varied in point of severity. Some of the cases were very obstinate, and did not respond well to treatment. The same symptoms developed in nearly all cases. The trouble began with an intense irritation, then an eruption appeared, resembling eczema, with a sort of a watery blister on the top. There was intense irritation all over the body, on the head, arms and limbs. I saw numbers and numbers of cases of this poisoning; I should say nearly a hundred cases in all came under my observation. The irritation seemed to remain, and was much worse than that caused by poison oak or poison ivy, and was not so easily gotten rid of. I treated most cases with some cooling application. Some cases were decidedly obstinate, but no case was serious enough to menace the life of the patient.

The Chemistry of it.

A great deal has been written in European works about the nettling properties of the brown-tail moth, and various conjectures made as to the cause of the trouble; but the general consensus of opinion seems to be that the nettling is caused by a poisonous substance in or on the finely broken hairs of the larvæ, coming in contact with the skin. Many also believe the cocoon to be even more troublesome than the larvæ. In an article in "The Entomologist," Vol. 17, p. 276, 1884, written from Chichester, Eng., it is stated that the moths of this species possess this stinging property, and the opinion is expressed that the irritation is caused by the white hairs that fringe the inner margins of the wings.

Mr. C. G. Barrett, in his excellent work on the "Lepidoptera of the British Islands," Vol. II., p. 294, 1895, writes as follows: —

With the silk composing the cocoon are interwoven the hairs of the larva, which becomes brittle, and, when the bush or hedge is disturbed, are thrown out as a fine dust, which, sticking to the skin of the hands, face or neck of a passerby, causes an intense irritation, with inflammation which closely resembles nettle-rash. It is on record that a thick hawthorn hedge upon which larvæ and cocoons have been abundant has retained for months the power of thus affecting any tender-skinned person rashly assaulting it with the beating-stick. Mr. H. Moncreaff noticed a larva rubbing its hairs across the scarlet tubercles on its back, and upon examination found at the base of each tubercle a valve, opening to a gland from which an oily substance exuded. This oily substance he found, on being applied to the skin, to produce at once inflammatory swellings, and all the irritation usually caused by contact with the hairs.

It is well known both to entomologists and to the layman that certain insects carry specific poisons, which when injected beneath the skin cause acute pain. Bees, wasps, mosquitoes, bedbugs and other insects fall in this class; and chemical investigations have shown that the poisonous principles are usually well-defined organic compounds, capable of being recognized by chemical tests. This being the case, it was at first supposed that the hairs of the caterpillars contained such a principle, and that the chemist of the gypsy moth committee, Mr. F. J. Smith, M.S., would soon determine its nature. A large amount of material, such as hairs, cocoons and molted skins, was submitted to Mr. Smith, who extracted them with various solvents with the following results, which we quote from Mr. Smith's notes:—

I made a number of extracts of the hairs with each of the reagents mentioned below, some of the extracts being of the hairs alone, others of the molted skins, and still others of the cocoons which contained hairs in great numbers. The reagents used were water, alcohol, ether, chloroform, petroleum ether, acetone, acetic ether, dilute sulphuric acid, dilute caustic potash. I tested each of the extracts after digesting for some hours, and in each case they nettled the skin. On the other hand, the *filtered* extracts (freed from the hairs) caused no irritation of any sort when applied even where the skin was broken. Careful chemical tests failed to show the presence of any organic acids or alkaloids. Hence I am led to believe that the irritation is of a mechanical nature, caused by the brittle, finely barbed hairs, and not due to a toxic principle.

Before submitting the material to Mr. Smith, we had already discovered that the irritation was not caused by the long barbed hairs (Plate 9, Fig. 5) nor by the white branching hairs (Plate 9, Fig. 1), but by the very minute barbed hairs which we call the nettling hairs, occurring in very great numbers on the subdorsal and lateral tubercles of segments 5 to 12 inclusive (Plate 9, Fig. 3), and also on the tubercle at the base of the long spines (Fig. 4). These nettling hairs are very small, only about one two hundred and fiftieth of an inch in length, very sharp at one end, and with two or three barbs at the other end and many along the sides. These barbs are so arranged that when these nettling hairs fall upon the skin any movement will cause them to work into the flesh.

The nettling of the skin may be caused by contact with the caterpillars in either of the last two molts, the cocoons, or to some extent with the moths, but contact is not necessary, as these fine nettling spines may fall or be blown by the wind. Cases are on record in England of travellers being affected when the wind blew strongly from infested hedges along the side of the road.

A careful examination of the caterpillars in each molt shows that the nettling spines do not occur except in the last two stages, or after the row of white spots appear along each side of the caterpillar. A great quantity of these nettling spines are always present scattered through the cocoon and more or less over the surface of the pupa, but in every case they appeared to have come from the last larval skin, and never to have developed from the pupa. An examination of a large number of moths of both sexes showed many of the nettling spines scattered over the surface of the wings and body in a very irregular manner, none of which were attached to the integument, but merely lodged among the hairs and scales of the imago. Only a few of the nettling spines were found on some specimens, while on others a large number occurred. In a few cases many of these spines were found in a confused mass in one spot, while on another not a single one occurred in that particular place. We must conclude, therefore, that as the caterpillar spins its cocoon these spines become scattered and lodge throughout the fabric, some of them falling on to the surface of the pupa after the last molt; and when the moth emerges and works its way out through the cocoon, more of these nettling spines are dislodged from it or from the molted skin and become entangled among the scales of the moth. This will explain the unequal distribution of these spines over the surface of the moths, and the reason why some possess the nettling properties much more than others. There is nothing in the structure of any of the scales or hairs on any part of the body or wings of these moths that could cause them to produce any nettling sensation.

Fallacies about the Insects.

As might be expected, many false notions prevail concerning the manner in which the insects cause the so-called poisoning. These fallacies are not confined to the average citizen, for even physicians, arguing from analogy, no doubt, have fallen occasionally into error on this point. It may be well to state, once for all, that the caterpillars do not sting, since nature has wisely denied them the apparatus for stinging, as that term is commonly understood; that they do not bite, for they have no beak such as is possessed by the mosquito or bedbug, while, from the anatomy of their tiny, blunt jaws, it would be impossible for them to cut through the human skin; that they do not eject a baleful venom, for they have neither the venom nor the means for ejecting it. Lacking all these attributes dear to the popular fancy, these insects, with their brittle, barbed hairs applied in affectionate contact to the human epidermis, still possess a means for making one truly long for a place "where moth and rust doth not corrupt."

Remedies.

The injury to the skin being a mechanical one, remedies must be sought among those materials which soften the skin and aid in the expulsion of the hairs. Of these, vaseline and sweet oil are among the best. Alcohol has been used with success, at least in giving temporary relief, while the same is true of the numerous coal-tar disinfectants now on the market. So prevalent is the dermatitis from the cater-

Plate 7.

Typical hair-covered egg masses of brown-tail moth; laid in July, 1899, on trees sprayed May 18, 1899, with arsenate of lead. So well did poison adhere that caterpillars died as fast as hatched.

Photo, Malden, Mass., Sept. 30, 1899.

THE BROWN-TAIL MOTH.

pillars in the metropolitan district in the summer months that druggists put out special lotions for the "brown-tail moth itch," many of which are meritorious.

LIFE HISTORY

The moths emerge from the cocoons from the 1st to the 20th of July, and fly principally by night. In marked contrast to the gypsy moth, the female brown-tail moth flies freely, and when caught up by the wind is often transported long distances. Mating takes place soon after the wings are developed, and egg laying begins a few hours later. The eggs are usually deposited on the under side of leaves on the outside of the trees, preferably near the top. The egg mass is much like that of the gypsy moth, although smaller and more elongated. It contains from two hundred to four hundred small globular eggs, thickly covered by a mass of brown hair from the tip of the abdomen of the moth. A typical egg mass (Plate 7) is about two-thirds of an inch long and about one-fourth of an inch wide. If the moths are disturbed while laying, or reach the edge of the leaf on which the eggs are being deposited, they often change the direction in which they move, or go to another place and recommence the work. Whenever such changes occur, the resulting egg mass is more or less irregular in form. Occasionally the eggs are deposited on branches and trunks of trees, on fences, on the walls of houses and even on lamp posts.

The Egg

The egg is honey-yellow in color, of a more or less globular form, being about one-thirtieth of an inch in diameter, and hatches in from fifteen to twenty days. The young larvæ feed at first on the leaf to which the egg mass was attached, but soon migrate to other near-by leaves, always returning at night to their original feeding place.

The Winter Web (Plates 2, 13)

The hibernaculum or winter web of this insect is of such a novel nature, at least to American entomologists, that a detailed description of it may well be given at this point.

In the fall the young larvæ feed upon the epidermis of the leaves only, causing them to turn as brown as though scorched by fire, and while still young commence the dwelling in which they hibernate during the winter (Plate 8). These winter webs of the brown-tail moth, constructed at the ends of the twigs, are from one to four inches in length and from one to one and one-half inches thick, depending upon the kind of tree on which they occur (Plate 6, Fig. 2). The insect readily adapts its style of architecture to the material at hand, making compact webs on pear and willow, and large open webs on maple and ash. Each web is composed of a tenacious silken hibernaculum, enclosing leaves from which the epidermis has been consumed, although the outer leaves on the web may not have been attacked. The webs are firmly attached to the twigs by stout bands of silk. Almost invariably the web commences where the egg cluster was deposited, and remains of it can usually be found on or in each web. Exit holes sometimes remain open on the webs throughout the winter, but as a rule they are closed by the matting together of the web under the influence of rain. The webs consist internally of numerous layers of silk, enclosing a great many small, irregular, silk-lined chambers, which are often connected, and contain from six to fifty larvæ. The usual number found in the chambers is about a dozen each. The larvæ are also often found in the galleries in the web. The lowest part of the web is usually full of fine black excrement, and the cast-off skins of the first molt occur in many of the chambers. Twenty winter webs of the brown-tail moth were opened Jan. 21, 1899, and their inmates carefully counted, the webs being dissected under a lens so that none of the insects might be overlooked. The webs contained respectively 253, 159, 253, 254, 223, 194, 182, 193, 84, 89, 47, 93, 299, 386, 674, 281, 664, 674, 802 (the latter being a double web), — a total of 5,804, or an average of 290 caterpillars per web.

The Larva.

The newly hatched larva is about one-twelfth of an inch long, with a shining black head, over the surface of which are a few pale brownish-yellow barbed hairs. These hairs

Plate 8.

Caterpillars of the brown-tail moth commencing to spin their winter web on a pear twig.

vary in length, but none of them are longer than the width of the head. The body is dull yellow, but this is obscured by the color of the tubercles, which are much darker than the ground color of the body, some of them being black. The tubercles are arranged as in the mature larva, and are armed with barbed spines like those on the head, except the subdorsal row, which has smooth, sharp-pointed spines, dark at the tip, lighter at the base, and about as long as half the diameter of the body. The length of this stage is from four to six days.

The larva after the first molt is about one-fifth of an inch long, with a shining black head, clothed with scattering pale brownish-yellow hairs, as in the preceding stage. The ground color of the body is dull yellowish, and the dark color of the tubercles is so pronounced as to give a darker appearance than in the preceding stage. The smooth, sharp-pointed spines of the subdorsal row of tubercles are no longer present, but are replaced by the ordinary barbed spines, and the subdorsal tubercles of the 5th and 6th segments are covered with a short, dense tuft of chestnut-colored feathery hair.

The larva after the second molt changes but little before hibernation, except in size. The head is black, and clothed with barbed brownish-yellow hairs. The body is dark brown, with two parallel longitudinal reddish-yellow lines between the subdorsal tubercles, extending from the head to the 10th segment, broken between the segments and also on the 5th and 6th segments by the tufts of hair, which are similar to those in the preceding stage. The coral-red retractile tubercles on the top of the 10th and 11th segments appear after the first molt, and are present in all the remaining larval stages, though at first they are of a light-yellow color.

The larvæ stop feeding and go into hibernation in their winter webs (Plate 14) early in September, some having molted once, others twice and a few three times.

Emergence in the Spring

The larvæ generally emerge from the hibernating tents from the 18th of March to the 20th of April, though the time varies somewhat, according to whether the season is early or late. The earliest record of emergence was by Mr. A. F. Burgess, who observed the young caterpillars emerging on March 18, 1898. By the last of April the larvæ are usually well at work, feeding on the unfolding buds of the pear and apple, while those on the elm and oak do not fare as well, since those buds open later in the season. The larvæ show but little method in feeding on the buds, simply burrowing into and often entirely consuming them.

So far as has been observed, there are three molts after emergence from the winter quarters before pupation. In the quiet state, just before the first molt in the spring, the larva is about one-fourth of an inch long, and differs only in size and in having the ground color of the body a little darker than it was before hibernation. They retreat into the winter web, where they remain quiet for twenty-four hours or more before molting.

The first molt in the spring occurs in about eight days after the larva emerges from the winter web, when it differs from the preceding stage in size, which is now about two-fifths of an inch in length; in the ground color of the body, now being a dark, smoky brown; and in having much longer spines, the longest of which are about three times the diameter of the body.

The second spring molt occurs about the middle of May, when the larva is about three-fifths of an inch long. This stage is similar to the preceding, except that the ground color and markings are more like those of the full-grown larva, though not nearly so bright.

The third spring molt occurs during the latter part of May, when the caterpillar is from three-fourths of an inch to an inch in length, and takes on the markings and characteristics of the mature larva. It now has for the first time the white branched hairs on the upper side of the lateral tubercles, on segments 5 to 12 inclusive, and the nettling hairs (Plate 9, Fig. 3) on the subdorsal and lateral tubercles of these same segments.

The fourth and last spring molt occurs in the early part of June, when the larva is from an inch to an inch and a quarter in length. The head is pale brown, mottled with

THE BROWN-TAIL MOTH.

darker brown, and has light-brown hairs scattered over the surface. These hairs are finely barbed, and similar in structure to the long ones arising from the tubercles of the body (Plate 9, Fig. 4). They are much shorter, however, the longest being half the width of the head. The basal segment of the antennæ and palpi is sordid white.

The body is dark brown or black, with numerous markings of a dull yellowish color, sometimes inclining to a dull reddish. These markings are as follows: the thoracic and anal shields, the latter often more or less dark brown in the middle, two parallel, irregular and more or less broken lines along the middle of the back, represented on the anterior segment by two rows of spots of variable size, a small space around each of the tubercles; many short, irregular, transverse streaks, most numerous on the sides and beneath. A cluster of reddish-yellow, finely barbed hairs of unequal length arises from each tubercle, while the sub-dorsal and lateral tubercles on segments 5 to 12 inclusive are thickly covered with fine barbed hairs (Plate 9, Fig 3), which give these tubercles a dark-brown color and the appearance of velvet, under a lens. These are the "nettling hairs." There is a fleshy, retractile, coral-red tubercle on the middle of the back of segment 11, and a similar one in the same place on segment 12. In one example these tubercles were abnormal in size and position, one being larger than usual, a little to the left of the dorsal line, and between segments 10 and 11, while the other was less than half as large as the first, and on the right side of the dorsal line, more than twice as far from it and slightly farther forward than the other.

The legs are dull reddish-yellow, with the claws and the outside of the basal segment black. The spiracles are vertically oval, and shining black. The surface of the body under a one-half inch objective has a shagreened appearance, with numerous fine, short hairs scattered over the surface.

The thoracic shield on the top of the 2d segment (just after the head) is wider in front than behind, and is divided by a transverse impressed line into two parts. Most of the hairs along the front edge incline forward over the head. They vary in length, the longest being about equal to the width of the head. Those on the posterior part of this shield are short, and sparsely scattered over the surface. A small tubercle occurs behind the outer end of the thoracic shield, and in line with the posterior part; the next is larger, oblique in front of the spiracle, and clothed with long hairs which incline forward more or less; the next tubercle is about half way between the last and the leg. The 3d and 4th segments have three tubercles on each side in an oblique row above the spiracular line, and two below. These two are represented on each of the segments of the body after the head, forming two subspiracular rows of tubercles. Above the spiracular line, on each side of segments 5 to 13 inclusive, are two large, round, nearly equal-sized tubercles, which may be called the subdorsal and lateral tubercles. The hairs on the head and other parts of the body are similar to those represented in Plate 9, Fig. 2, and the long ones in Fig. 5, except those of a clear white color (Plate 9, Fig. 1) on the upper side of the lateral and a few on the outside of the subdorsal tubercles, on segments 5 to 12 inclusive. These hairs form a row of eight lunate white spots along each side, which is the most striking characteristic marking of the caterpillar.

The larvæ spin their cocoons and pupate during the last half of June, remaining in this stage about twenty days. A favorite place for pupation is the leaves at the tips of the branches, and not unfrequently a dozen or more larvæ assemble and spin a common web, within which each caterpillar forms its own cocoon and transforms into the pupa. Another favorite place is under fences and beneath the edge of clapboards. In 1897 Mr. Kirkland saw a mass of cocoons nearly two feet across in the cornice of a house on Vine Street, Somerville.

The cocoons are composed of grayish silk, so loosely constructed that the pupa may be readily seen through it. The pupa is about five-eighths of an inch long, of a dark-brown color, with a conical spine at the end of the abdomen, this spine being armed with a cluster of minute hooks at the extremity. There are smooth, yellowish-brown hairs scattered over the abdomen and top of the thorax, but none on the antennae, leg or wing covers.

The Moths

As already noted, the moths emerge from the pupal stage from the 1st to the 20th of July, the time varying, according as the season is early or late. In 1898 the height of the flying season was July 16, in 1899 it was July 8, while in 1902 it was July 14. They are essentially night-flyers, only a few being seen on the wing in the day time, while the others remain at rest on the trees, fences and under side of leaves. In an hour or two after sunset a few of the moths venture forth, the number increasing as it grows dark, and from 10 o'clock till midnight the moths fly in the greatest numbers.

The average expanse of the wings of the males is one and three-tenths inches, and of the females an inch and a half. Head, thorax and wings snow white, antennae white above, with the under side and pectinations yellow, abdomen, above, smoky brown, more intense posteriorly. On the end of the abdomen of the female is a large globular tuft of hairs, which in different lights shade from golden yellow to dark brown. In some females the hairs of the under side of the head, thorax and abdomen are tinged more or less with pale yellow. This is more pronounced in the males, where, on the under side of the head, pectus and costa of the fore wings, it is dark brown.

In July, 1897, a quantity of cocoons and pupae was gathered and placed in a large glass-covered box, the moths being removed as they emerged. The following table shows the relative proportion of the sexes : —

DATE.	Males.	Females.
July 7,	5	2
8,	12	8
9,	41	38
10,	153	135
11,	32	46
12,	64	54
13,	61	100
14,	21	53
15,	9	12
16,	–	–
17,	1	3
Totals,	399	451

Seven female moths which had not deposited their eggs were killed and carefully dissected. They were found to contain eggs as follows: 344, 300, 217, 286, 257, 145, 209, — a total of 1,758, or an average of 251.1 per moth.

DISTRIBUTION.

The principal distribution of the brown-tail moth takes place at the time when the female moths are on the wing. These insects fly freely, and have a habit of soaring upward above the tree tops and buildings. When the moths in their nocturnal flights have thus risen in the air, they are often drifted by the wind over long distances. An excellent illustration of the distribution of flying moths by air currents was given by the high wind prevailing July 12–14, 1897, — a time when the flying season of the brown-tail moth was at its height in Somerville and Cambridge. A few weeks previous the caterpillars had swarmed in multitudes in these cities, and in due time the white-winged moths emerged in myriads. So plentiful were they at this time that arc lights

Plate 9.

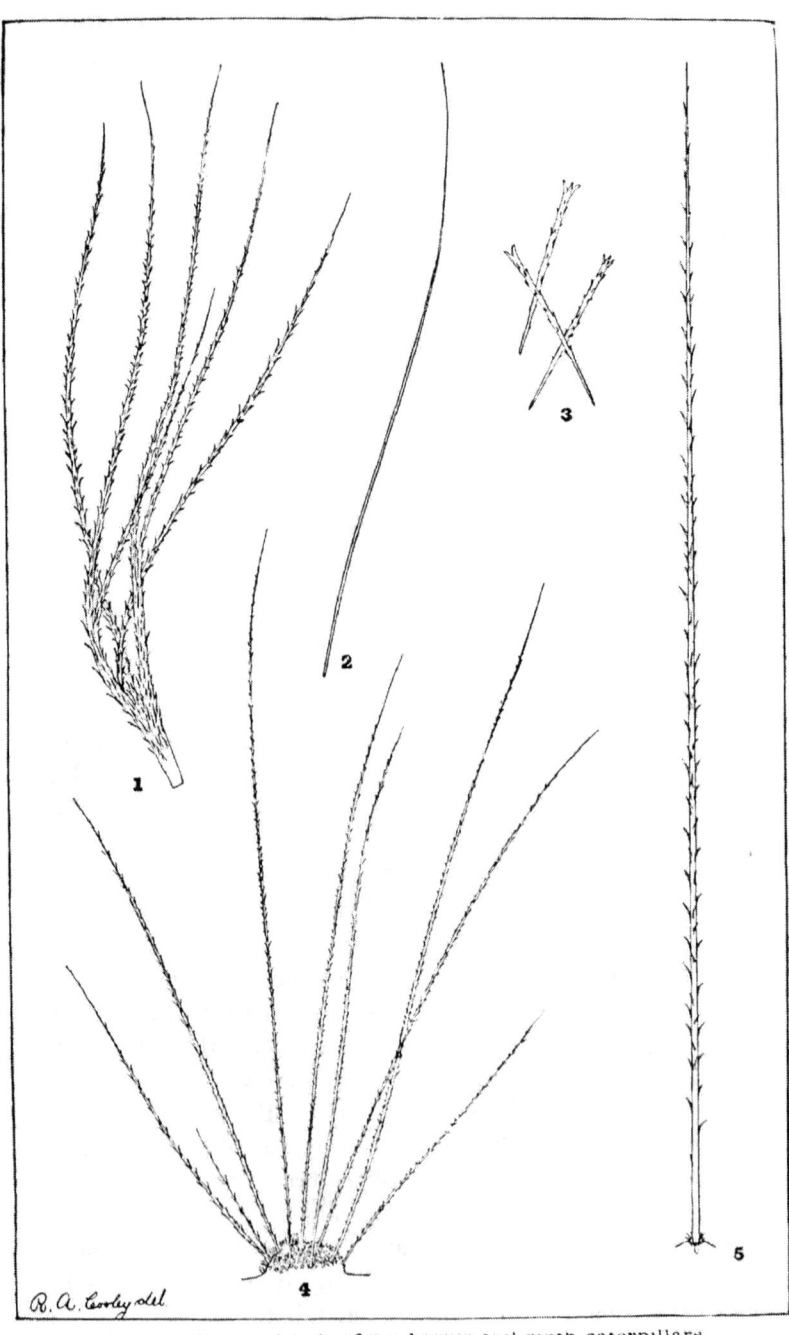

Various forms of hairs from brown-tail moth caterpillars.

around which the insects hovered seemed indeed to be the centres of miniature snow-storms. While the moths were swarming on the night of the 12th, the wind came fresh and strong out of the south to south-west, blowing steadily at the rate of twelve to sixteen miles per hour. After midnight it increased in velocity to twenty miles an hour at 2 A.M. (July 13), twenty-five miles an hour at 8 A.M., twenty-eight to thirty miles an hour at noon, thirty-five miles at 5 P.M., and reached the maximum velocity of forty miles an hour late in the afternoon. By midnight the gale had decreased to fourteen miles an hour, but increased again rapidly, reaching a velocity of twenty miles an hour at 2 A.M., July 14, and forty-eight miles an hour at 8.40 A.M., then decreased to thirty miles at noon and twenty miles at 6 P.M. The day movement of the wind is not important, as the moths are nocturnal, but it was soon apparent that the wind of the nights of July 12 and 13 had transported the flying insects into many cities and towns lying to the northward, while to the south the distribution was limited. Some two or three years were necessary before the increase of the moth in the new localities was sufficient to call attention to its presence but by the fall of 1899 it had been found scattered from Somerville northward to the State line at Methuen and eastward to Seabrook, N. H., — a point some forty miles distant from the original colony. In the spring of 1902 the nests of the moth could be seen easily from the car windows in every town along the eastern division of the Boston & Maine Railroad from Boston to Portsmouth, N. H. The occurrence of the moth at Kittery, Me., was reported in 1899 by the late Prof. F. L. Harvey, Orono, Me. The Kittery occurrence was doubtless due to the transportation of household goods from a badly infested Somerville estate at a time when the insect was in the cocoon stage. Recently, Prof. James Fletcher, the distinguished Canadian entomologist, has reported the occurrence of the mature moth at St. John, N. B. In the absence of evidence to the contrary, he believes that the insect was transported on the steamers plying between Boston and St. John. This view is a logical one, for the trees on the islands in Boston harbor and along the north shore are generally infested by the brown-tail moth. It is entirely probable that moths attracted by the bright lights fly to and alight on passing vessels, and in this way the insects already may have been carried accidently to many seaports. The danger of spreading the moth by shipping is of course greatest on the coastwise steamers, where the boats make landings before the moths have laid their eggs and died.

When the moths are flying, they are strongly attracted to light. In tracing the distribution of the moth in the winter of 1898-99 it was found that the most promising places to search for the insect were in the centres of population, where electric and other lights were massed in greatest numbers. It is not difficult to understand how the swarming insects driven by the wind from the place of emergence fly onward to the nearest mass of light. This tends to bring about the infestation of the central portions of cities and towns before the pest finds its way to the outlying residential or farming districts.

Again, the flying moths enter brightly lighted electric and street cars. At the flying season warm weather is the rule, and open car windows give the insect easy entrance. Mr. Kirkland has repeatedly seen the female moths in rapidly moving electric cars and on two occasions in local railroad trains.

Aside from the principal means of distribution mentioned, it is necessary to consider the dropping of caterpillars on teams, and the danger from nursery stock grown in the infested district and shipped to customers living at a distance. In common with other caterpillars, the brown-tail moth larvæ have a habit of spinning down on silken threads from their feeding places, and hanging for some time suspended in the air. Where they are feeding on street trees, they are frequently intercepted by passing teams and are thus carried from place to place. In the very thorough studies of the distribution of the gypsy moth made by Mr. E. H. Forbush some years ago, it was shown that one of the chief aids in spreading the moth was the regular continued traffic of milkmen, grocers and others. The spinning habits of the brown-

Plate 10.

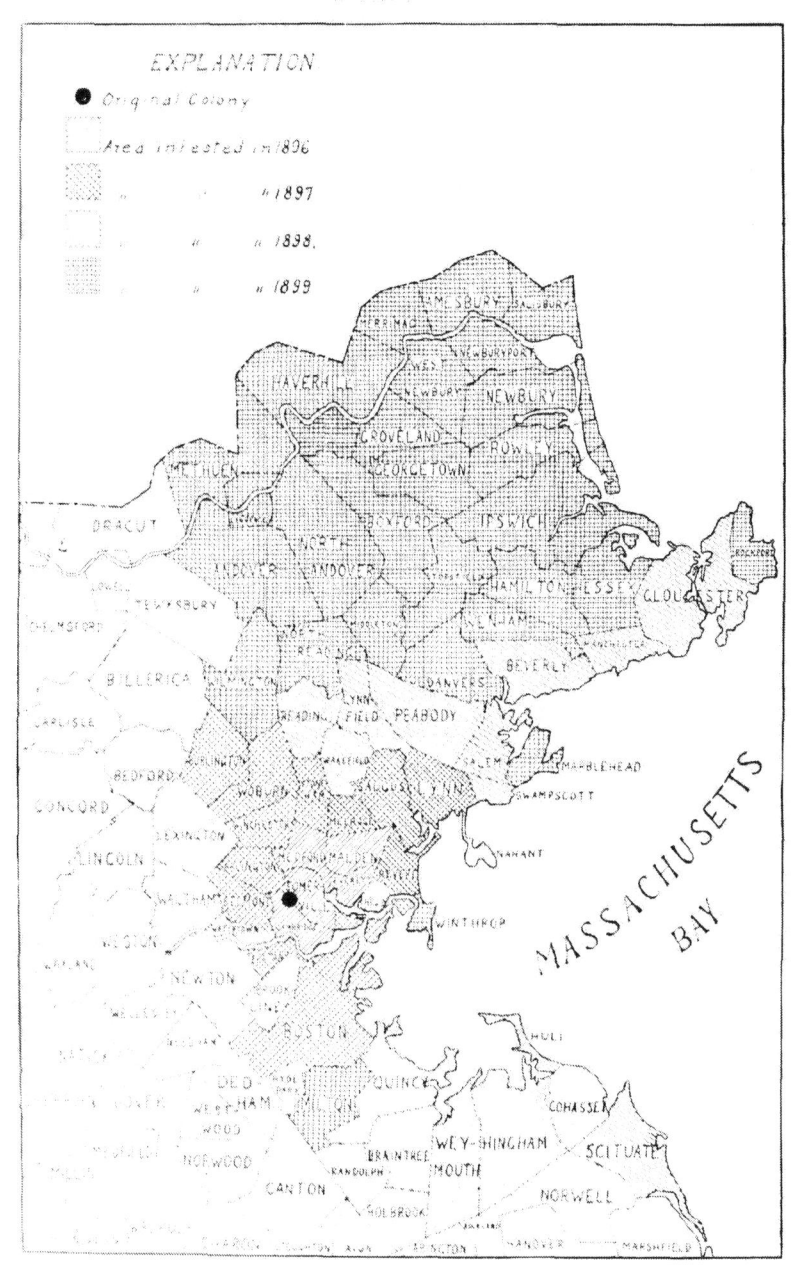

Map showing the rapidly increasing spread of the brown-tail moth.

tail moth do not differ materially from those of the gypsy moth, and its distribution by teams is doubtless of frequent occurrence.

Several eastern Massachusetts nurseries are more or less infested by the brown-tail moth, and there is constant danger that a small caterpillar web may be sent out with trees to some distant locality, and there establish a moth colony. This matter is one that has received special attention from the efficient State Inspector of Nurseries, Dr. H. T. Fernald; while the proprietors of infested nurseries are taking every precaution to insure the destruction of moths on their grounds and prevent its spread elsewhere.

At the present writing the moth is known to occur in Massachusetts at Scituate on the south, westward to Brockton, Hudson and Stow, northward to Methuen and eastward to the sea. The occurrences at Kittery, Me., and St. John, N. B., have been mentioned. South-eastern New Hampshire is also generally infested, and we fear in the course of a few decades the pest will have found its way over the greater part of New England. The neglect of a moth colony on an infested estate results in the spreading of the pest to adjoining places; neglect on the part of generally infested towns leads to the swarming of the moth and its dispersal into neighboring municipalities. The ease with which the moth becomes distributed gives an additional reason for thoroughness in stamping out incipient colonies.

The tabulation below gives a good idea of the rapidly increasing spread of the insect. Since 1899 no accurate records of the distribution of the moth have been kept. The area infested in 1896, the year previous to the discovery of the moth, was determined by the finding in the spring of 1897 of the winter webs of the previous year.

	Square Miles
Area infested, fall of 1896,	29
Area infested, fall of 1897,	158
Area infested, fall of 1898,	448
Area infested, fall of 1899,	928
Area infested, fall of 1902, estimated,	1,500

NATURAL ENEMIES.

One reason why the brown-tail moth is so very injurious in Massachusetts is found in the lack of the parasitic enemies which hold the insect more or less in check in its original home. As yet our native parasites have not adapted themselves to this new caterpillar, and, freed from the checks that control it at home, it here causes a greater and longer-continued damage than is common in Europe. Of the Hymenopterous parasites common to caterpillars of this class, *Pimpla tenuicornis* Cr. and *Phaeogenes hebe* Cr. have been bred in some numbers from the cocoons. The greatest natural aid in destroying the brown-tail moth seems to be the tiny parasite *Diglochis omnivora* Walk. Large numbers breed in a single pupa, and, emerging early in the season, attack other larvae and pupae, and thus prevent their development into moths. From a single pupa 158 *Diglochis* were obtained in July, 1898, while from a mass of about four quarts of cocoons over three thousand of these parasites emerged during the same month. Of the dipterous parasites, the only one determined is *Euphorocera claripennis* Macq. So far as we have observed, the caterpillar is only slightly attacked by parasites of this class.

The number of predaceous bugs which assemble on trees infested with the brown-tail moth early in the spring is quite remarkable. These bugs, hibernating in sheltered localities, eagerly seek food in the first warm days of spring. The brown-tail moth caterpillar is the largest insect of its kind which is at all abundant early in the season, and the predaceous bugs readily adapt themselves to it. The result is greatly to the advantage of the bugs and to the farmer. May 1, 1899, with the thermometer in the shade at 90° F., six trees infested with the brown-tail moth were examined, with the result that the following number of predaceous insects were found feeding upon the small caterpillars: 113 *Podisus serieventris*, 36 *Podisus placidus*, 2 *Milyas cinctus*, 1 *Lutropis humeralis*, 1 wasp, *Polistes pallipes*; in other words, on the six infested trees there were 152 predaceous bugs at work destroying the larvæ, or an average of 25.2 bugs to a tree. Many of the bugs were mating, and it was not unusual to see two bugs both feeding on a single larva. The wasp made a business of tearing into the webs, extracting the larvæ, rolling them up into a ball by means of the fore-feet and jaws, and carrying them off.

In the spring of 1899 Mr. Kirkland placed three webs of the brown-tail moth on as many wild cherry trees in rear of his house at Malden, with a view to studying the habits of the caterpillars, the locality being already somewhat infested. As soon as the larvæ emerged and commenced to feed, predaceous bugs of the genus *Podisus* appeared, and in less than a fortnight had completely wiped out each caterpillar colony.

The humble toad must also be reckoned in the list of the enemies of the brown-tail moth. During the early summer, when the caterpillars are swarming, large numbers are eaten by toads. Seven toads taken on infested estates May 24-26, 1897, contained respectively 7, 5, 0, 3, 8, 3 and 12 brown-tail moth larvæ. The work of toads is more noticeable, however, during the flying season, when they assemble under arc lamps, and devour the fluttering moths as they fall stunned or injured from the lamps above. Four toads taken under arc lamps at Somerville on the night of July 16, 1897, contained respectively: 11 male moths, 4 female moths; 6 male moths, 4 female moths; 7 male moths, 4 female moths; 9 male moths, 8 female moths.

Bats also are worthy of mention among the natural enemies of the moth. Where the moths swarm thickest around the lamps, the bats are constantly in evidence, their noiseless work being easy to trace by the falling of white moth wings. At Malden, on the night of July 14, 1898, several bats were noticed destroying the moths around an arc light. The following morning over two hundred wings of the brown-tail moth were counted on the ground beneath that particular lamp. Allowing four wings to each moth, this would indicate the destruction of fifty imagoes by the bats at this one point.

It occasionally happens that the young hibernating caterpillars are destroyed early in the fall by a fungus or mold which develops in the webs. The caterpillar destruction from this cause is most noticeable during a fall that is especially damp and rainy; we have never noticed it taking place in a dry fall. It is most common in those webs which are spun on trees with large leaves, such as the maple or horse-chestnut. These webs are of necessity more open than those spun on trees with smaller leaves, such as the pear or willow. The rain penetrates these larger and more open webs, and dampens the masses of excrement which are found in many of the chambers of the web. It is evident that when these webs become thoroughly dampened inside, the molding and death of the caterpillars usually occur.

Electric Lights.

Although electric lamps can hardly be classed among the "natural" enemies of the moth, they exercise none the less a very important influence in destroying the swarming moths during the flying season. We have pointed out in another place how these lamps, by attracting the moths, materially increase their distribution. It is well to show, therefore, the good done by the lamps in destroying the swarming insects. The moths come out in large numbers soon after the lights are turned on, and from ten o'clock to midnight the swarming is at its height. The moths encircle the lamps at times in such numbers as to somewhat obscure the light. The bodies of those killed by the electric current drop continually, and by morning the ground under the lamps in the worst-infested regions is liberally sprinkled with bodies of dead moths. Counts of dead moths under five arc lamps were made at four o'clock in the morning on July 16, 1897, with the following results: lamp No. 1, 236 males, 71 females; lamp No. 2, 29 males, 11 females; lamp No. 3, 7 males, 4 females; lamp No. 4, 3 males, 4 females; lamp No. 5, 22 males, 2 females.

Lamp cleaners report that they often find a quart or more of dead moths in the lamps early in the morning. Mr. Kirkland spent several nights in 1897-98 watching the swarming of the moths, and found that towards morning many of the

Plate 11.

Damage by tiny caterpillars of brown-tail moth in fall.
Photo, Medford, Mass., Sept. 18, 1899.

arc lamp globes would become more or less clogged by the bodies of the insects. As soon as daylight breaks, however, the English sparrows swarm to the lamps and feed upon the moth bodies. They also carry them to their young. A remarkably short time suffices for these birds to remove a quart or more of the moths from the lamp globes. While the old birds evidently enjoy the moths as a morning meal, they also carry them in large numbers to their young.

Birds as Destroyers of the Brown-tail Moth

Birds play an important role in checking the spread of the brown-tail moth. While their attacks are perhaps more conspicuous while the insect is in the moth stage, it is probable that the greatest number of insects are destroyed in the larval form, at which time many species of birds not only consume the caterpillars, but carry them to their young. Armed as these larvae are with an abundant growth of nettling hairs, it would seem that they would prove distasteful morsels for the birds, and be largely protected from their attacks. This, however, is not the case; the same species of birds that feed on other hairy caterpillars, such as the tussock moth, forest tent caterpillar or gypsy moth, readily adapt themselves to the brown-tail moth caterpillars. Of the birds feeding on the caterpillars, the yellow-billed and black-billed cuckoos and Baltimore oriole are worthy of special mention. They are common visitants to infested trees, feeding freely on the insects, and carrying them to their young. They arrive in their summer migration when the caterpillars are about two-thirds grown, and make repeated visits to the infested trees, feeding particularly on the masses of insects clustered for molting. As is well known, the cuckoos are formidable enemies of hairy caterpillars. Their services in destroying the common tent caterpillar of the orchard are of highest value, and alone should entitle them to the good-will of the farmer or property owner, and this statement is also true of the Baltimore oriole. Of the other birds which feed on the larvae, the yellow-throated vireo and blue jay are worthy of special mention.

It is however, when the moths are emerging that the layman notices more particularly the work of birds in checking the increase of this insect. The white moths leave their cocoons and remain in situations more or less exposed until their wings have developed. As a result of the habit of the caterpillars in spinning their cocoons in a common mass there will often be a large number of moths within a small area on a fence, house wall or other sheltered locality. The birds soon locate these favored spots, and often consume the moths even before their wings have expanded. In this work of moth destruction the kingbird and some of the flycatchers figure to a limited extent, but the most formidable enemy of the mature moths is the notorious English sparrow. That this bird, whose evil habits in driving out native insectivorous birds are so well known, should show this distinctly beneficial trait, may be a matter of surprise to many students of nature, but the fact remains that the English sparrow, with its numerous progeny, exerts a great and beneficial influence in checking the moth in our thickly settled districts, — places where natural checks are often most deficient.

July 16, 1897, the time when the moths were notably thick at Somerville and Cambridge, Mr. Kirkland observed whole flocks of English sparrows following along the line of fences and carefully searching for the moths, which when found were greedily devoured. The sides of the pickets and even the bottom of the rails were carefully examined by these sharp-eyed moth hunters, and all moths of either sex found were consumed.

The sparrows do not confine their attentions to hunting for live moths, but also act as scavengers in removing from the arc lamps the masses of moths which accumulate in the globes over night. At 10.30 P.M., July 14, 1897, an arc lamp at Malden around which the moths were swarming was from one-fourth to one-third full of the dead bodies of the moths. Wishing to make a count of the number of moths thus destroyed by the lamp, Mr. Kirkland visited it at 5.30 the following morning, but at that hour the sparrows were actively feeding on the moths in the lamp globe, and also carrying them to their young. July 16 other arc lamps were examined at 1.30 A.M., but even at that time the birds had anticipated the observer, and were carrying off the moths in large numbers. At 5.30 the sparrows had emptied the globe of moths, and also consumed the insects on the ground underneath it. It was observed at 4.30 that there were sixteen male and two female moths on the lamp pole, but at 6 A.M. the birds had consumed all of them.

On the afternoon of July 16, at a time when the moths were still emerging, a drive through the worst-infested districts showed only three brown-tail moths on lamp poles or tree trunks. There were plenty of the moths in sheltered places in the trees and under the leaves of rank herbage on the ground, but those in conspicuous positions had been destroyed.

Below is given a list of birds known to feed upon the brown-tail moth in any of its stages: —

Yellow-billed cuckoo.	Red-eyed vireo.
Black-billed cuckoo.	Yellow-throated vireo.
Kingbird.	Black-and-white warbler.
Blue jay.	Chestnut-sided warbler.
Baltimore oriole.	American redstart.
Rose-breasted grosbeak.	Chickadee.
Indigo bird.	American robin.
Scarlet tanager.	English sparrow.

Food Plants.

That the favorite food of the brown-tail moth is the pear tree is very unfortunate, since there are few places in the United States where pears are more successfully cultivated than in eastern Massachusetts, — indeed the pear orchards of Revere and Arlington have a reputation not limited by State boundaries. Next to the pear the apple is preferred by the caterpillars, although they breed freely on stone fruits, and also on the elm, maple and several species of oak. When the caterpillars swarm forth from overcrowded colonies, they seem to exercise but little selection in the matter of food, but feed generally upon all deciduous trees, on many shrubs and even upon herbage. A list of plants upon which the caterpillars have been found feeding is given below: —

Barberry, — *Berberis vulgaris.*
Basswood, — *Tilia Americana.*
European linden, — *Tilia Europaea.*
Horse-chestnut, — *Æsculus Hippocastanum*
Sugar maple, — *Acer saccharinum.*
White maple, — *Acer dasycarpum.*
Cut-leaved maple, — *Acer dasycarpum,* var *Wieri*
Red maple, — *Acer rubrum.*
Box elder, — *Negundo aceroides.*
Variegated box elder, — *Negundo aceroides,* var *variegata.*
Stag-horn sumach, — *Rhus typhina*
Smooth sumach, — *Rhus glabra*
Smoke tree — *Rhus Cotinus*
Locust, — *Robinia Pseudacacia*
Beach plum, — *Prunus maritima.*
Wild red cherry, — *Prunus Pennsylvanica*
Choke-cherry, — *Prunus Virginiana*
Damson plum, — *Prunus domestica*
Purple-leaved plum, — *Prunus Pissardi*
Apricot, — *Prunus Armeniaca*
Japanese plum, — *Prunus Japonica.*
Meadowsweet, — *Spiraea salicifolia.*
Thimbleberry, — *Rubus occidentalis.*

Dwarf wild rose, — *Rosa lucida.*
Rose, — *Rosa nitida.*
Choke-berry, — *Pyrus arbutifolia.*
Pyrus pinnatifida.
English hawthorn, — *Crataegus Oxyacantha.*
Paul's thorn, — *Crataegus coccinea,* var. *Pauli.*
Cockspur thorn, — *Crataegus Crus-galli.*
Shad bush, — *Amelanchier Canadensis.*
Quince, — *Cydonia vulgaris.*
Japan quince, — *Cydonia Japonica.*
Common red currant, — *Ribes rubrum.*
Black currant, — *Ribes nigrum.*
Gooseberry, — *Ribes grossularia.*
English gooseberry, — *Ribes Uva-crispa.*
Witch hazel, — *Hamamelis Virginiana*
Flowering dogwood, — *Cornus florida.*
Cornus mas.
Arrowwood, — *Viburnum acerifolium.*
Arrowwood, — *Viburnum dentatum*
Black haw, — *Viburnum prunifolium*
Weigelia rosea
Aster puniceus
Sweet pepperbush, — *Clethra alnifolia.*
White ash, — *Fraxinus Americana.*
Red ash, — *Fraxinus pubescens.*

Blue ash, — *Fraxinus quadrangulata.*
Black ash, — *Fraxinus sambucifolia.*
Common lilac, — *Syringa vulgaris.*
Japanese lilac, — *Syringa Japonica.*
Slippery elm, — *Ulmus fulvus.*
White elm, — *Ulmus Americana.*
Cork elm, — *Ulmus racemosa.*
English elm, — *Ulmus campestris.*
Scotch elm, — *Ulmus montana.*
Red mulberry, — *Morus rubra.*
Tartarian mulberry, — *Morus Tartarica.*
Sycamore, — *Platanus occidentalis.*
Black birch, — *Betula lenta.*
Yellow birch, — *Betula lutea.*
White birch, — *Betula populifolia.*
Paper birch, — *Betula papyrifera.*
Cut-leaved birch, — *Betula alba,* var. *laciniata.*
Hop-hornbeam, — *Ostrya Virginica.*
White oak, — *Quercus alba.*
Swamp white oak, — *Quercus bicolor.*
Red oak, — *Quercus rubra.*
Scarlet oak, — *Quercus coccinea.*
Black oak, — *Quercus coccinea,* var. *tinctoria.*
Pin oak, — *Quercus palustris.*
Scrub oak, — *Quercus ilicifolia.*
Chestnut, — *Castanea sativa,* var. *Americana.*
Blue beech, — *Carpinus Caroliniana.*
American beech, — *Fagus ferruginea.*
Purple beech, — *Fagus sylvatica,* var. *purpurea.*
Crack willow, — *Salix fragilis.*
White willow, — *Salix alba.*
Weeping willow, — *Salix Babylonica.*
Heart-leaved willow, — *Salix cordata.*

Remedies.

Web Destruction.

In the case of the brown-tail moth, action looking to the prevention of damage by the caterpillars is of more importance than the application of remedies after the insects have commenced feeding. With this insect the traditional "ounce of prevention" is worth many "pounds of cure." For nearly six months, or, generally speaking, from the first of October to the first of April, these insects are massed together within their silken winter webs. These webs, as already pointed out, are attached to the tips of the twigs, are grayish-white in color, and easily seen when the foliage has fallen from the trees. In the case of either fruit or shade trees of ordinary size, nothing is easier than to cut off and burn the webs. The success of this operation was early discovered, and European treatises on the moth make particular mention of this method for combating it. The well-known European laws concerning the brown-tail moth lay particular stress upon this destruction of the winter webs, and, in fact, it is the essential feature of the famous French law of "*echenillage*."

For the work of web destruction there will be required ladders of suitable length, stout clothing, and some form of pruning shears attached to a long handle, the so-called "Waters pruner" being the one generally used. It has been found that this work can be done more rapidly and thoroughly by two men, one on the ground to discover and point out the webs, the other cutting them off while in the tree. All webs removed in this manner should be carefully gathered in bags or baskets, and destroyed by fire. A careful series of experiments made at the insectary of the gypsy-moth committee in the winter of 1897–98 showed that, if these webs are left upon the ground, the vitality of the insects is not destroyed by the action of the elements, and that a considerable percentage of them will emerge unharmed the following spring. In this experiment, as conducted by Mr. Kirkland, a number of brown-tail moth webs were spread upon the ground in a single layer in the fall, and covered with a piece of coarse poultry netting; thus the webs were exposed throughout the winter to rain, snow, freezing and thawing. The following spring, as soon as the caterpillars in webs on fruit trees near by began to show signs of activity, the webs were taken from the ground (April 15, 1899) and each placed in a glass-covered box. The larvae commenced to emerge soon after the webs were brought into a warm room, and continued to come out until April 22. April 26, as no more larvae came from the webs, they were destroyed. In all, 19 webs yielded larvae, while from 82 webs no larvae emerged. Careful records were kept of 8 webs from which caterpillars emerged, in order to determine the number of larvae coming from each web. The results are tabulated below: —

Plate 12.

Fall web worm and brown-tail moth contrasted. On left, loose open web of web worm; on right, compact web of brown-tail moth.
Photo, Malden, Mass., Aug. 9, 1899.

	April 19.	April 20.	April 21.	April 22.	April 23.	April 24.	April 25.	April 26.	Totals.
No. 1,	16	3	7	4	–	–	–	–	30
No. 2,	2	6	3	13	–	1	–	–	25
No. 3,	–	–	17	70	–	10	1	–	98
No. 4,	–	–	10	11	–	12	–	–	33
No. 5,	–	–	2	–	–	–	–	–	2
No. 6,	–	–	16	–	–	–	–	–	16
No. 7,	–	–	–	2	–	–	–	–	2
No. 8,	–	–	–	5	–	–	–	–	5
Total,	–	–	–	–	–	–	–	–	211

This gives us an average of 26.3 larvæ per web emerging unharmed; the average normal web contains about 290 larvæ.

It is preferable, where circumstances permit, to burn the webs in a furnace or stove, thus insuring their complete destruction. Where the webs are burned in a bonfire in the field, it often occurs that a part become covered with ashes and are not consumed. In a case noticed by one of the writers, some years ago, a number of webs that had been partly scorched in a bonfire were still found to contain living insects. Silk is an excellent non-conductor of heat, as well as of cold; and in this case, while the webs protected the caterpillars from the rigors of winter, they also preserved a part of them unharmed from the action of fire.

Spraying.

There will always be cases where the work of web destruction has been neglected, from one cause or another, — too often from the indolence of the property owner. When the caterpillars emerge in the spring and commence feeding on the young buds and leaves, the best remedy is to spray the tree promptly and thoroughly with arsenate of lead, using 3 or 4 pounds to 50 gallons of water. The insecticide should be thoroughly applied to the leaves, particularly in the part of the tree where the insects are feeding. In cases where trees cleared of the caterpillar webs stand near infested trees, they may also be preserved from damage by the migrating caterpillars by a thorough spraying, as above indicated. Where arsenate of lead cannot be obtained, Paris green may be used, at the rate of 1 pound to 150 gallons of water, keeping the mixture well agitated while spraying. In the case of shade trees, this spraying should be done as soon as the foliage develops, and the same rule holds good with fruit trees, where the insects are abundant. If the trees are not badly infested, however, it is often desirable to wait until after the blossoms have fallen before spraying, thus securing a double benefit by destroying the caterpillars of the brown-tail moth, and also preventing damage to the fruit by the codling moth.

Where neither the web destruction nor early spraying has been practised, it often occurs that the caterpillars, nearly full grown, are found devastating the foliage of the neglected trees. Where the insects are nearly mature, spraying with arsenical poisons does not always give satisfactory results, for the reason that a great many of the insects disturbed by the spraying will pupate without feeding longer. In such cases it is more satisfactory to prepare a quantity of strong kerosene emulsion, then jar the caterpillars from the trees by beating the latter with poles. The insects falling to the ground should be thoroughly drenched with the kerosene emulsion, applied either with a sprayer or from a watering-pot. Trees freed from the caterpillars in this way, and also non-infested trees standing near those on which the caterpillars are feeding, may be easily preserved from damage by banding them with some sticky material, such as the German raupenleim, or its American substitute, bodlime, or even with tar or printer's ink. These materials, properly applied, form a sticky band over which the insects cannot pass.

Banding.

In using tar or printer's ink, it is best to first apply a small band of cotton waste or wool, then tack over it a band of tarred paper, to which the ink or tar is applied directly. These bands should be repainted at intervals of a few days, until the caterpillar season has passed. The bands of lime (either raupenleim or bodlime) are applied directly upon the bark. The bands should be from two to three inches wide, one-half inch thick at the bottom, tapering upward to the bark, in order to shed rain. The bottom of the band should be shaped to form a sharp shoulder. It is the tendency of insect lime to yield up a small quantity of oil under the influence of the sun, thus keeping the lower edge of the band always moist and sticky, and presenting an insurmountable barrier to the insects.

When the insects have pupated, the cocoons may be gathered and destroyed, although this work is usually attended with a severe nettling of the skin, described in another place. Cocoons and pupae thus gathered should be placed in a barrel covered with mosquito bar, so that the parasites contained in them may escape, while the moths' will be unable to pass through the netting. In the case of the brown-tail moth this precaution is an excellent one, as this insect is extensively parasitized in the pupal stage.

Second Brood.

It often occurs in badly infested localities that the small caterpillars hatching from the eggs occur in sufficient numbers to partially or entirely defoliate the infested trees This damage does not occur on trees which have been thoroughly sprayed with arsenate of lead the preceding summer. Where the insects are numerous, a fall spraying with arsenate of lead is recommended, except in the case of trees in fruit, since, where the fruit is within a few weeks of ripening, it is not advisable to use the very adhesive as well as very poisonous spray. (Plate 11.)

Insecticides

For the work of spraying the foliage, no poison is more effective than the arsenate of lead. This material is of light specific gravity, hence remains well suspended in the spraying solution, and insures an even distribution on the foliage. It does not kill quite as quickly as Paris green, but is very effective against the insects when used in the proportions directed. It has two special advantages, in that it sticks to the foliage tenaciously throughout the season, and will not scorch or injure the most delicate leaves. It is slightly more expensive than Paris green or London purple, if the first cost of the material only is considered. On the other hand, as one spraying is often sufficient to preserve a tree unharmed from leaf-eating insects for an entire season, while repeated sprayings of Paris green are necessary, the arsenate of lead often proves the cheaper insecticide.

How made

Arsenate of lead may be prepared by dissolving separately 3 parts commercial nitrate of lead and 1 part commercial arsenate of soda, and pouring the two solutions together, when the arsenate of lead is flung down as a dense white precipitate. This formula is based upon the average grade of nitrate of lead containing 66.5 per cent. lead oxide, and arsenate of soda containing 59.8 per cent. arsenic oxide. Owing to the difficulty in obtaining these chemicals in small quantities at a fair price, and the uncertainty as to their purity, the small user will do well to purchase some one of the prepared forms of arsenate of lead now offered in the market, instead of attempting to manufacture the insecticide. Owing to the increasing use of arsenate of lead for spraying purposes, several reliable manufacturers have put it upon the market in the form of a paste, which is ready for use as soon as water is added, thus being at once convenient and inexpensive.

If Paris green is used, a strength of 1 pound to 150 gallons of water will give good results, and the proportion of poison should not be greater than 1 pound to 100 gallons,

Plate 13.

Winter webs of brown-tail moth on English oak.
Photo loaned by Chas. Bradley, Supt. Farm School, Thompson's Island.

otherwise burning of the foliage will occur. In using Paris green, it should be borne in mind that this insecticide has a high specific gravity and settles rapidly in the spraying tank, hence it should be stirred continually while being applied

Kerosene emulsion, useful in destroying caterpillars jarred from trees, and on fences, walks, etc., is made by dissolving ¼ pound hard soap in 2 quarts of water, and adding to the solution, while hot, 1 gallon of kerosene oil, stirring the whole, or pouring it rapidly from one pail to another until a stable white emulsion is formed. This emulsion for use on the caterpillars should then be diluted at the rate of 1 part emulsion to 5 of water. At this strength there will be some injury from the kerosene to grass and other foliage, but the effect on caterpillars will be more satisfactory than where the normal dilution of 1 part to 9 of water is used.

Apparatus.

The damage by the brown-tail moth is as severely felt in proportion to the value of the crop in the kitchen garden as on the farm. In fact, owing to the scarcity of native insect-eating birds in our cities, injury by caterpillars of this class is sometimes more severe in cities than in the open country. While the city owner requires the same spraying materials as are used on the farm, his needs in the line of apparatus are much less.

For use in a kitchen garden or on a small estate, excellent results in spraying can be obtained from a brass syringe, such as is commonly used in greenhouses for showering plants. A suitable syringe can be bought for about $4, and by its use vegetables and fruit trees of good size may be sprayed satisfactorily.

On larger estates, and particularly where shrubbery has a prominent place, no outfit is more convenient and generally useful than a copper knapsack spray pump. We might add that nothing is more wearisome to the flesh than to carry one of these outfits on a hot day, but such labor often pays big dividends. The writers would advise against the purchase of galvanized-iron knapsacks; these soon rust out, two years being about the limit of their usefulness. On the other hand, a copper knapsack pump, costing at the start about $12, if properly cared for will last ten or fifteen years. It is important that it be thoroughly washed with clean water after using.

In orchards and for general work against the brown-tail moth and other insects, a substantial spray pump, mounted on a 50-gallon cask, is a necessity. Such a pump should have brass working parts, an effective agitator, and an air chamber of ample capacity to equalize the flow of the spray. The price of pump and cask ought not to exceed $12 or $15. In addition will be needed 50 to 100 feet white cotton hose, costing about 10 cents per foot, an 8 or 10 foot spray pole extension, $1; and a Vermorel nozzle, 60 cents, — these figures being approximately correct for present market conditions. If desired, the spray pole can be made by any plumber from a piece of one-fourth-inch gas pipe. At the lower end a hose nip (reducer) should be inserted to receive the end of the hose; the other end should be threaded to screw directly into the nozzle.

For extensive spraying operations, such as are necessary in large orchards, parks, and especially where tall shade trees are to be sprayed, larger and stronger pumps will be required. In these operations it is often desirable to use two or more lines of hose, often against a head of seventy-five to 100 feet. A pump suited for this work must have cylinders of ample capacity, a large air chamber and a rigid frame and base. From $25 to $30 will cover the cost of such a pump. Other details will be about as follows: suction hose, fittings, strainer, etc., $5; 200 feet hose, $20; two spray poles, $2; two nozzles, $1.20; 150-gallon hogshead, $1.50. An outfit of this class is suited for the largest spraying operations, such as park or city work, as well as for extensive orchard sprayings. At Dedham, Ipswich, Bridgewater, Lawrence and elsewhere street elms have been sprayed with outfits of this description, with highly satisfactory results.

Plate 14.

Winter webs of brown-tail moth on American elm and rock maple, Medford, Mass., Nov. 20, 1899.

How to Spray.

One might suppose that the spraying of a tree or a plant was a simple operation, requiring but a modicum of skill and intelligence. This view doubtless is responsible for a large part of the failures in spraying, for particular care and attention must be given both to the mixing and the application of the insecticide materials, in order to obtain satisfactory results.

Assuming that the proper materials in proper quantities have been obtained and mixed according to directions, a suitable outfit provided, and the water used carefully strained, the work of spraying may be commenced.

Where trees are treated, spraying should commence at the top. If the wind is blowing, the work should be carried on from the windward side. Often in a breeze of low velocity large trees can be thoroughly sprayed from the windward side alone, the mist being drifted on the air.

The spray should be applied as a fine mist, never in a stream. The dew remains on the leaves, the rain runs off. The same is true of spraying, a mist adheres, but drops run off. The nozzle should have a very small aperture, and, if backed by a pump of adequate power, the spray will burst forth as a fine mist, which should be allowed to diffuse in the air before striking the foliage. Hence it is desirable to hold the nozzle a few feet from the leaves to be treated. In all cases spraying should cease as soon as the foliage begins to drip.

Spraying Experiments

Numerous experiments with insecticides on brown-tail moth larvæ were carried on at the insectary of the gypsy moth committee. So thoroughly, however, had this field of experimentation been covered in the case of the gypsy moth, that few additional facts of value were discovered. Certain field experiments upon the brown-tail moth caterpillars are of particular value, however, as showing results obtained under the actual conditions which confront the property owner having infested trees.

In May, 1898, there were secured for experimental purposes a large number of pear trees, from ten to fifteen feet high, standing on an estate in the southern part of Malden. These trees were thoroughly and quite uniformly infested with the brown-tail moth, and the caterpillars had emerged and commenced feeding, being at the time of the experiments in the second and third molts. In each case these trees were sprayed with various insecticides, as given below. In the case of arsenate of lead, the quantities mentioned represent the actual dry arsenate of lead contained in the ingredients used.

Field Experiments*

1. Arsenate of lead, 1 pound to 150 gallons of water —

May 19	sprayed	May 27,	90 per cent dead
May 20	no results	May 28,	— —
May 21	no results	May 29,	— —
May 22	ceased feeding	May 30,	— —
May 23	50 per cent dead	May 31	— —
May 24	— —	June 1,	— —
May 25	— —	June 2	all dead
May 26	— —		

2. Arsenate of lead, 2 pounds to 150 gallons of water —

May 19	sprayed	May 27,	90 per cent dead
May 20	no results	May 28,	— —
May 21	no results	May 29,	— —
May 22	ceased feeding	May 30	— —
May 23	50 per cent dead	May 31,	— —
May 24	— —	June 1	— —
May 25	— —	June 2,	all dead
May 26	— —		

3. Arsenate of lead, 5 pounds to 150 gallons of water —

May 19	sprayed	May 25	— —
May 20	no results	May 26	— —
May 21	no results	May 27	— —
May 22	ceased feeding	May 28	— —
May 23	80 per cent dead	May 29,	all dead
May 24	—		

4. Arsenate of lead, 10 pounds to 150 gallons of water —

May 19	sprayed	May 23,	80 per cent dead
May 20	no results	May 24,	— —
May 21,	few dead	May 25,	— —
May 22	80 per cent dead	May 26,	all dead

* The per cent arsenate of lead used in these experiments is equal to about ... the commercial arsenate of lead paste.

5 Paris green, 1 pound to 150 gallons of water —

May 19,	sprayed	May 26,	. 70 per cent dead
May 20,	no results	May 27,	- -
May 21,	no results	May 28,	- -
May 22,	10 per cent dead	May 29,	90 per cent dead
May 23,	50 per cent dead	May 30,	- -
May 24,	- -	May 31, .	- -
May 25,	- -	June 1, .	. all dead

6 Scheeles green, 1 pound to 150 gallons of water —

May 19,	sprayed	May 27,	- -
May 20,	no results	May 28,	- -
May 21,	no results	May 29,	75 per cent dead
May 22,	5 per cent dead	May 30,	- -
May 23,	25 per cent dead	May 31,	- -
May 24,	- -	June 1,	95 per cent dead
May 25, .	-	June 2,	- -
May 26,	. 50 per cent dead	June 3,	all dead

In the fall of 1898, while the newly hatched caterpillars were still feeding, a number of trees at Malden were sprayed with arsenate of lead at the rate of 12 pounds to 150 gallons of water. As the webs were nearly formed at this time, it seemed desirable to keep a certain number of them, to determine whether the poison had killed all of the caterpillars. Later, in April, 1899, the webs were placed in a warm room and isolated, with the following results: —

243 webs on pear —

April 26	4 webs yielded larvæ
April 27	25 webs yielded larvæ
April 28	5 webs yielded larvæ
April 29,	- webs yielded larvæ
April 30,	- webs yielded larvæ

34, or 14 per cent

A number of webs had also been gathered under exactly identical conditions from certain large elm trees that had been sprayed as thoroughly as possible at the same time and with the same strength of poison. These webs yielded many more larvæ as will be seen by the table below —

237 webs on elm —

April 26.	101 webs yielded larvæ
April 27.	10 webs yielded larvæ
April 28.	12 webs yielded larvæ
April 29.	— webs yielded larvæ
April 30.	3 webs yielded larvæ

126, or 53 per cent

These figures show clearly that fall spraying is not an exterminative method, probably for the reason that some of the insects enter the webs early to hibernate. It is also very interesting to notice the difference in the effectiveness in the spraying of large and small trees. The pear trees were easily reached by ladders, and thoroughly sprayed. On the large elms thorough work was also attempted and much time and labor spent in spraying them, but the results were only one-fourth as satisfactory. These figures also have a wider significance, in showing us how difficult it is to get entirely satisfactory results in spraying large trees.

Municipal Work.

The advent of the brown-tail moth in Massachusetts and its gradual distribution in thickly settled districts gives another excellent illustration of the interdependence of all citizens in a community where matters of public good are at stake. Where the moth occurs but scatteringly, its ravages are slight and the pest is easily controlled. The case is far different, however, when the insect is numerous; one single pear or apple tree on an estate may carry from one to two hundred webs, each web containing, on the average, two hundred and fifty caterpillars. The insect spreads readily in the taller shade trees, from which it can only be cleared at a great expense. Even if the property owner succeeds, at the outlay of much time and money, in freeing his place from these insects, his labors are unavailing should his neighbor, through ignorance or carelessness, allow the trees on his estate to remain badly infested.

We have seen repeatedly in the metropolitan district numerous illustrations of the annoyance and damage thus caused by the neglect of one property owner to clear his trees from the insects after his neighbors had destroyed the webs on their own trees. This matter of web destruction is often an expensive undertaking. Many property owners can ill afford it; certainly tenants cannot, as a rule; while the non-resident owner is very apt to neglect this work. Clearly, then, this is a case where co-operation is a necessity, if the moth is to be held in check; and, lacking State supervision of the work, municipal enterprise offers the most promising means of relief.

Under our present laws, municipal officers have the power to enter on private estates for the purpose of suppressing dangerously injurious insects, and it is the opinion of the writers that the control of the brown-tail moth clearly falls within the field of legitimate municipal enterprises.

This pest is certainly a menace to the property and wealth of citizens, while by its attacks on street trees it directly destroys the property of the city or town where it occurs. The good of the community demands that the brown-tail moth should be suppressed, and in no way can this be done more economically than through the direct and systematic work of some municipal department, preferably the one having in charge the parks or streets. In this way all tax payers in a community, sharing, as they do, in immunity from damage by the moth, also share in the cost of its suppression.

A campaign against the brown-tail moth is best begun in the fall or early winter, preferably in December, after the leaves have fallen from the trees. A preliminary scouting or examination of the territory is always of advantage, as showing where the moth is thickest, and the amount of work necessary for its suppression. If the municipal appropriation is of adequate amount, the whole region should be carefully worked over, and all webs destroyed, in order to prevent the local increase of the moth and its further spread the following summer. Where, as is too often the case, the appropriation is a limited one, the worst infestations should be attended to in a thorough manner. It is but folly to spend money clearing tall street trees from the webs of the caterpillar while in adjacent yards there stand pear trees bearing hundreds of webs within easy reach. Dense infestations should be stamped out first of all, to prevent a serious caterpillar outbreak the following year, with its consequent damage to property and persons. Later on, the more thinly infested districts should be worked over so far as funds permit.

From three to ten men can be profitably employed in a gang, while several gangs may be placed under one foreman or inspector. Maps showing accurately the location of the principal infestations, together with the streets included therein, should be in the hands of the foreman, in order that a proper record of each day's work may be made, and thus preserved for future reference.

The importance of destroying the moth on private estates as well as on street trees has already been pointed out. Usually where this has been attempted by municipal authorities it has met with the approval if not co-operation of property owners. Since, however, previous to 1902 there was no law authorizing municipal authorities to enter private grounds for this purpose, a special act conferring the desired authority upon them seemed desirable. The following law was enacted Feb. 5, 1902:—

[CHAPTER 57, ACTS OF 1902.]

AN ACT TO AUTHORIZE CERTAIN CITY AND TOWN OFFICERS TO ENTER UPON PRIVATE LANDS FOR EXTERMINATING THE BROWN TAIL MOTH AND OTHER SIMILAR PESTS.

Be it enacted, etc., as follows:

SECTION 1. Whenever the brown tail moth, the elm-leaf beetle, or any other tree or shrub destroying pest shall be discovered in any city or town of the Commonwealth, such city or town, by the principal officer or officers to whom the care of the shade trees on the streets or roads of such city or town is or may be intrusted, may enter upon private land for the purpose of investigating said pest and may adopt reasonable measures to prevent its spread and to secure its extermination.

SECTION 2. The owner of any land so entered upon, who shall suffer damage by such entry and acts done thereon under the authority herein given, may recover the same of the city or town in which the lands so asserted to have been damaged are situated, by action of contract, but any benefits received by such entry and the acts done on such lands in the execution of the purposes of this act shall be determined by the court or jury before whom such action is heard, and the amount thereof shall be applied in reduction of said damages.

SECTION 3 Whoever shall oppose the entry aforesaid, or obstruct the performance by the said local authorities of said work shall be punished by a fine not exceeding twenty dollars for each offence.

Hecki Kirkland
Moth.

SMITHSONIAN INSTITUTION LIBRARIES

3 9088 00220164 8

nhent QL561 L9F36
The brown-tail moth, Euproctis

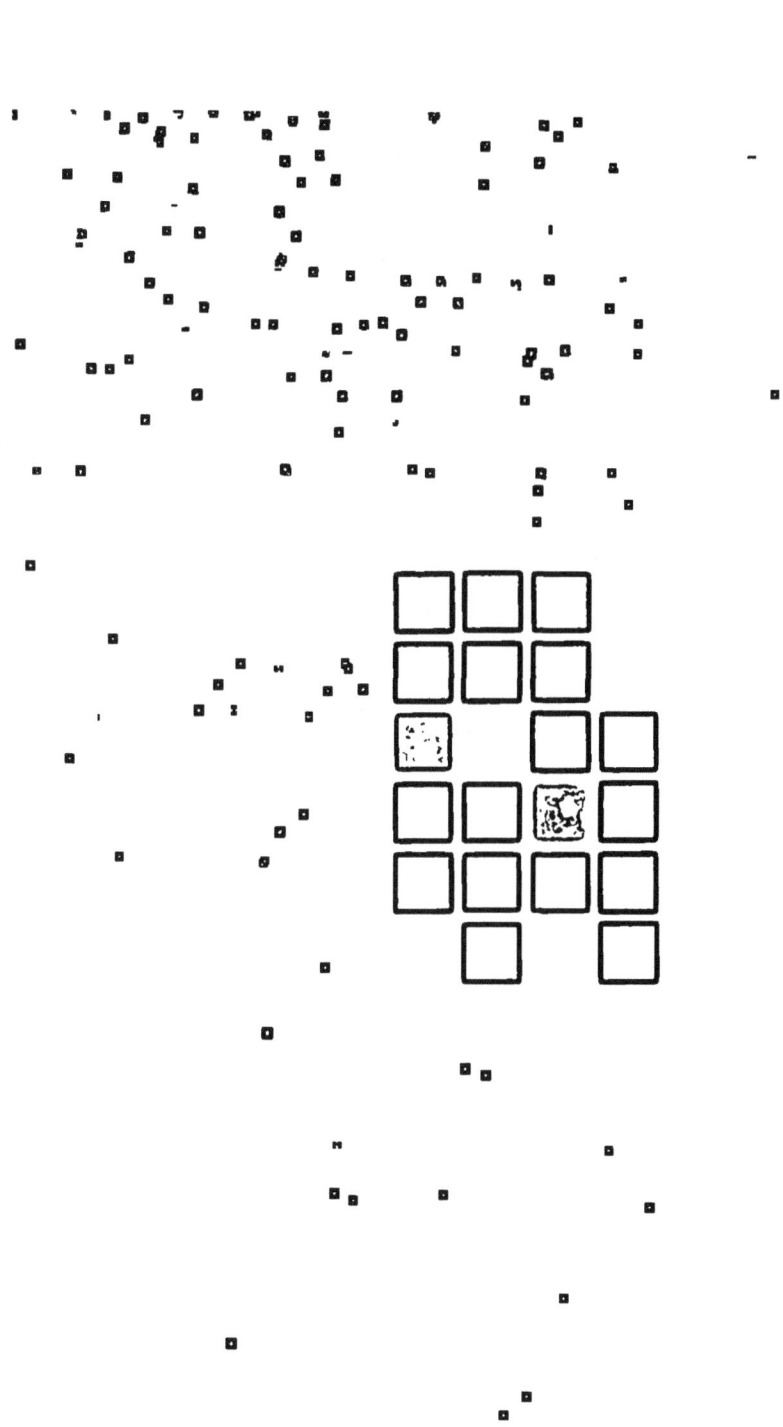

CPSIA information can be obtained
at www.ICGtesting.com
Printed in the USA
BVHW042312121220
595588BV00032B/620

9 781360 790022